TIES *that* BIND

a 52-week devotional for
mothers and daughters

KRISTIN ARMSTRONG

New York Boston Nashville

THE HOLY BIBLE, NEW INTERNATIONAL VERSION®, NIV® Copyright
© 1973, 1978, 1984, 2011 by Biblica, Inc.™ Used by permission. All rights
reserved worldwide.

FaithWords
Hachette Book Group
237 Park Avenue
New York, NY 10017

www.faithwords.com

Printed in the United States of America

RRD-C

First Edition: November 2013
10 9 8 7 6 5 4 3 2 1

FaithWords is a division of Hachette Book Group, Inc.
The FaithWords name and logo are trademarks of Hachette Book Group, Inc.

The Hachette Speakers Bureau provides a wide range of authors for
speaking events. To find out more, go to www.hachettespeakersbureau.com
or call (866) 376-6591.

The publisher is not responsible for websites (or their content) that are not
owned by the publisher.

Library of Congress Cataloging-in-Publication Data

Armstrong, Kristin.
  Ties that bind : a 52-week devotional for mothers and daughters / Kristin
Armstrong.—First Edition.
    pages cm
  ISBN 978-1-4555-2902-5 (hardcover)—ISBN 978-1-4555-2900-1 (ebook)
1. Mothers and daughters—Prayers and devotions.   I. Title.
BV4847.A765 2013
242'.6431—dc23

                    2013017541

I dedicate these pages to the generations of women in my life who have shaped me and guided me, and the legacy we create together. The ties that bind us are sacred and secure.

For my grandmothers, Aune and Mildred. I lost both of you in the process of writing this book, and the ache is fresh. I hope to honor you every day of my life.

For my mother, Ethel. Your heart and your wisdom are all over these pages. I love well because I have been well loved. Thank you, Mom.

For my daughters, Isabelle and Grace. I wake up every single day and want to be a better woman because you are my girls. I love you with all my heart, always.

Thanks be to God for his indescribable gift!

2 Corinthians. 9:15

My mother, wearing braids made
by my grandmother.

ACKNOWLEDGMENTS

I would like to thank my editor, Jana Burson, and my publisher, Rolf Zettersten, at Hachette Book Group. The only thing better than doing work you love is doing work you love with good friends.

I would like to thank the inner circle of mothers and daughters I know and love who took the time to preview these pages and give me heartfelt feedback and inspiration. I appreciate you more than you know.

I would like to thank my Bible study sisters. We've raised our children side by side for over a decade now, and I am blessed to make this journey together. Thank you for your encouragement, wisdom, accountability, humor, and most of all, your prayers.

INTRODUCTION

Ah, yes. Mothers and daughters. What could be more powerful, more fierce, more fragile, more fraught with emotion and layers of meaning than the relationship between a mother and a daughter? Every single woman bears the legacy, and sometimes the scars, of this most intimate tie.

Ultimately we are the product of our relationship with God. But the foundation we have with our family has a great deal to do with how we see ourselves along the way. Some mother-daughter relationships are healthy and joyful, some are broken, some are passive-aggressive, some are guilt-ridden, and some represent total abandonment. The healing and wholeness we have sought, or haven't, impacts our ability to mother, our daughters' ability to mother, and on and on for generations. Our relationship with our mother impacts our friendships, our marriages, and our mothering. It colors the way we view all our relationships with women. Are we healthy and free? Or are we competitive? Demanding? Hurtful? Withdrawn? Judgmental?

We struggle in relationships with our toddlers, our adolescent girls, our teenagers, our girls leaving home, our girls getting married, our girls as they parent our grandchildren. We get stuck in our relationships with our mother-in-law and our daughters-in-law. We resort to old patterns that have never worked for us in the past because we don't always seek God's wisdom in these timeless relationships. Our love is complicated (*I need you/Leave me alone*). We need God's word to help us grow up and into free and beautiful relationships. As painful as it is for daughters to pull away and grow, it is equally painful for mothers as they endure the separation. What if we relied on God to help us learn to understand and love ourselves—and each other—better as we grow up and grow old?

That is my hope for this book, to explore where we've been, where we are, and where we want to go. This book represents a yearlong journey, intended to be taken together. Each week we will delve into a new area, and hopefully, with God's help, we will reach deeper levels of understanding, communication, and healing.

Mothers have braided their daughters' hair for generations, and in that simple act of love we can see that a cord of three strands is not easily broken (Eccl 4:12). As we weave our relationships with our daughters with a third strand, our faith in Christ, our ties to each other will be healthy and strong.

God's Word never returns to Him void. Let's open our hearts and minds and allow Him to work on us. The femininity of our family, the legacy of our love, the genuineness of our generations is at hand—His hand.

With great love and anticipation,
Kristin

TIES *that* BIND

Mother

> Love the LORD your God with all your heart and with all your soul and with all your strength. These commandments that I give you today are to be on your hearts. Impress them on your children. Talk about them when you sit at home and when you walk along the road, when you lie down and when you get up.
>
> *Deuteronomy 6:5–7*

There is no better place to start than here. This is explicit instruction on how to begin to forge a relationship with God—love Him with everything you've got. To love Him, you have to get to know Him, and that is exactly what we are going to do together this year.

Embedded in these verses are also some explicit instructions on parenting. I just love how God put this here, up front in His manual, so to speak. As God's rules, or His commandments, are laid out, He makes it quite clear to parents that it isn't enough that we imprint these laws on our hearts. We are also called to impress them upon our children. Which means that we know them well enough to teach them and live them well enough to represent them. This is a huge undertaking, a powerful call. If it feels enormous, it should, because it is.

The passage goes on to explain when we should impress these commandments on our children. Let's think for a second about our culture and our frenetic lives today and how our pace impacts our parenting. We are supposed to share God with our children when *we sit at home*, when we *walk along the road*, when we *lie down* and *get up*. I don't know about you, but I don't sit at home very often at all. And I rarely walk along the road. And I sure as heck don't have time to lie down unless I'm about to pass out at bedtime. Talk about a gut check. I am going to revisit pace this year. I'm going to be intentional about sitting down, about taking a child with me and walking our dog, about taking time to rest, snuggle, and take a day off more often than just when someone is sick.

If we are struggling to share our faith with our daughters, perhaps we need to really read God's Word here and see how our rushing is affecting our communication and our level of intimacy with our children. Hurrying will never yield the depth required to make soul-level connections.

This week, as we start off together, let's begin by slowing down. If we're going to go deeper and do things differently with our daughters this year, we have to start with some new habits. Let's stop multitasking and make a point to sit, go for a walk, or lie down together. This week, let's honor God and His commandments by forging ahead with just these changes. They may seem like small things, but their impact is eternal.

Daughter

> Love the LORD your God with all your heart and
> with all your soul and with all your strength.
> These commandments that I give you today are to
> be on your hearts. Impress them on your children.
> Talk about them when you sit at home and when
> you walk along the road, when you lie down and
> when you get up.
>
> *Deuteronomy 6:5–7*

Loving God with all your heart, soul, and strength does not just happen. Loving someone like that requires that you know Him deeply. God wants that kind of relationship with you. He wants you to know all about Him: His history, His promises, and His truth. He wants to be the first person you go to when you have a problem or have great news to share. He wants to take your worries and be the first person you thank when things turn out okay.

How are you going to get to know God like that?

We're going to get to know Him together this year, one week at a time. We're going to look deeper into the Bible together and see how God's Word is meant for you.

In order to learn more about God's character, you can turn to His Ten Commandments. Make a point this week to sit down with your mom and talk about God's laws and how they might apply to you and your life right now. Or go for a walk together and use that time outside to talk about God. Each commandment goes deeper than just what it says. For example, *thou shalt not kill*. Okay, easy enough, right? You think to yourself, *I'm not a murderer, so I'm all good. Check.* Not so fast. How often do you kill someone's good mood, someone's hope, or someone's spirit with your words or actions? Really think about it. Or, *thou shalt not put any gods before me.* You can think, *I love only one God, so that's not a problem for me. Check.* Wait a minute here. What about the "gods" we can make of our friends, our social life, our weight, our clothes, or our abilities at school or in sports? Yep, keep going. Each commandment can go deeper and deeper until you get to the root of how each law fits with your heart and in your life right now.

This is exactly where we want to go in order to build a strong foundation with God. Ask Him to show you the areas where you have room to grow, and ask Him to send His Holy Spirit to help you get there. He will reveal the same things to your mom, and you will both have work to do. But it's good work, the kind of work that brings peace and understanding.

Connecting with God takes time. And a life of rushing from one thing to the next doesn't leave enough time. How can you slow life down this week and make room to learn about God?

Mother

> ... "That is enough," the LORD said. "Do not speak to me anymore about this matter."
>
> *Deuteronomy 3:26*

I can totally relate to God the Father here, having been to that "enough is enough" place with my children countless times. Moses, blessed as he was, must have been somewhat taken aback by such a firm refusal from God.

There have been times that I have prayed, fervently and fiercely, thinking that my heart was right and my request was certainly in line with God's will, and yet, God said no. It can be painful to pour our hearts out to God in prayer, especially on behalf of our children, only to receive a negative response. For faith that is new or has not been tested in this way, it can be extremely disheartening—even to the point that we are tempted to turn our back on God in our anger, sadness, or disappointment. This is a crisis of faith, and precisely the moment that we must remind ourselves that we do not have the answers and, try as we might, we cannot see the bigger picture. We don't know what lies ahead, what chips must fall in order for this life to be affected this way, another life this way, all interconnected and all according to an intricate timeline we simply cannot fathom. His thoughts are higher than our thoughts and His ways higher than our ways (Is 55:8–9).

My mentor helped me to understand a deeper perspective to God's no. She reminded me that in the garden of Gethsemane, Jesus prayed in agony for a different path, for the cup of sorrow to be taken from Him. And God refused *His own Son*—His spotless, sinless Son. Jesus obeyed, all the way to the cross. And because of God's no and the obedience of Jesus to follow the path prescribed for Him, we receive the forgiveness and healing of the cross and are restored into relationship with God for eternity. Imagine if God had granted Jesus' request? Imagine if Jesus had refused to pick up His cross and labor on? Where would we be?

Suffering is bigger than us, and it unites us in ways we cannot fully comprehend in this lifetime. When God says no, He may actually be saying yes to something far greater, far more important than we are able to know. We have to trust Him in spite of the way things seem at the time, in spite of circumstances, in spite of our own feelings sometimes. It's easy to trust God when things are smooth and our prayers are blessed with yes. But how deep is our trust when the tides of our life turn?

Are you fighting or begrudging the noes in your life? Can you open your heart to the possibility that God is working on something big for you? (Jer 29:11)

Daughter

> ... "That is enough," the LORD said. "Do not
> speak to me anymore about this matter."
>
> *Deuteronomy 3:26*

When I was younger and growing in my faith, I prayed to God and presented my needs and requests to Him, and He usually answered my prayers. I would often pass my test. I was able to repair a friendship. Maybe I made a certain team, or we won a big game. All these things helped build my faith, and I started going to God for more and more help, in big and small things.

But what happens when we ask God for something important to us and He is quiet—or worse, He responds with a very obvious no?

This can be very confusing. We might feel angry with God. We might be so disappointed that we don't want to talk to Him. We might start to think maybe He isn't real, and maybe all the times He seemed like He was there for me—maybe it was just a coincidence that things somehow worked out? If we aren't careful, we can let God's no cause us to pull away and stay away. Things happen that are so hard to understand. Parents get divorced, people die of cancer, we fail a test or a class, or our friends turn their backs on us. Why does God let us hurt if He loves us so much?

This question is a hard one when you're young, but guess what—it doesn't get any easier to understand when you're older! Adults struggle with the same things.

A friend reminded me that Jesus did not want to be turned over to the authorities and sent to die on a cross. In fact, in the garden of Gethsemane, He begged God to figure out another way. But God said no to His own Son. So if God says no to Jesus, He certainly may say no to us.

But think about this: If Jesus had not obeyed God and taken His cross, where would we be? Because He died for us, we are free today, and we have eternal life in heaven. There is so much more going on behind the scenes; we have no idea.

When God tells you no, it's okay to be upset, but don't pull away. Express yourself and your disappointment to God, but be open to His plans. They are often far better than what you originally had in mind. We cannot see what He sees. Be patient and trust Him. He loves you and will take care of you no matter what.

Can you think of a time you prayed and did not get what you wanted? How did you feel? Did you eventually end up with something better, or are you still waiting? Keep the faith.

Mother

> … "It will be good for you, my daughter, to go with the women who work for him, because in someone else's field you might be harmed."
>
> *Ruth 2:22*

What is better than good girlfriends?

Good, godly girlfriends. That's what. There is nothing like faithful friends. They will laugh with you, pray with you, encourage you, forgive you, teach you, reprimand you when you need it, and form a fortress around you when life's storms come. It is crucial to pray for godly friends for your daughter if she doesn't have them, or pray for protection of these precious relationships if she does have them.

No matter what we have poured into our girls, there comes a time when they are not with us all the time. They go off to school, off with friends, off to play sports, off to college, and eventually there will be more influence from their peers than from their home. This is precisely why we want them to be surrounded with friends who believe and share their values. We have to pray, but we also have to be proactive.

What does this look like? Well, first, we cannot offer a vision of something that we are not living ourselves. We each must examine our own inner circle to know if we are surrounded by God's girls. We must make a priority to value these relationships in our lives, in front of our daughters. I want my girls to see me going to Bible study, to retreats, and to church with my friends. I want them to feel the powerful network of praying women who love them and know their hearts. Second, we have to help them build a foundation of these relationships for themselves. We can help them connect at church, find Bible studies, and foster experiences with other believers. We cannot force them to need or nourish these relationships, but we can help our girls to distinguish the difference between varying levels of intimacy between friends. Friends who share faith are bound by a cord of three strands, and these are the relationships that stand the tests of time and trial.

Take time this week to examine the quality of your friendships. What does your daughter see when she witnesses you and your girlfriends? How can you help her foster Christ-centric connections or build on the ones she already has?

These are the relationships that will yield solidarity and security. Pray for wisdom. Pray with gratitude. Pray with perseverance. Pray for God's girls.

Daughter

> ... "It will be good for you, my daughter, to go with the women who work for him, because in someone else's field you might be harmed."
>
> *Ruth 2:22*

It's hard enough these days to figure out friendships. Girls can be fickle, can't they? One minute you are in the group; the next, you aren't sure. Some girls change friends as often as they change clothes. This can be confusing, and sometimes painful.

How do you learn to grow the friendships that you can trust and rely on?

God tells us here in the book of Ruth that it's a good idea to go with His girls. This means friends who believe in Him and value the things that He values. This does not mean that you cannot be friends with people who don't share your faith—not at all. In fact, God wants us to reach out and share His love with others. But it does mean that when you are choosing your closest confidantes, you should choose the ones who will best care for your heart. Often these are the girls who believe that you should love God first, and then love your friends like you love yourself.

Friendships grow differently when they are rooted in God. They don't hog the sunshine and the rain from one another, but they give each other space and grace to grow and bloom. They maintain the trust between them. They honor the plans and promises they make. They tell each other the truth. They have each other's backs instead of talking behind them. They forgive each other when hurts invariably happen instead of holding grudges.

Going with His girls means that you can travel safely in a pack. You have His protection and His provision with you. Remember, God tells us that He is present any time two or more are gathered in His name (Mt 18:20). This means *all the time*, if you are with a friend who believes.

This week, think of how you can seek out or improve relationships with faithful friends. Talk to your mom about her close friendships throughout her lifetime. Be mindful of asking God about the safest people to trust and forming friendships in which you can completely be yourself without fear or judgment. When in doubt, or when you have a choice, go with His girls.

Mother

> **Contend, LORD, with those who contend with me...**
>
> *Psalm 35:1*

The mama bear version of this verse has to be "Contend, O Lord, with those who contend with my children." Amen?

It is so tempting to want to fight our daughters' battles for them. Just today one of my girlfriends said that she would give *anything* to save her daughters from even one second of the body image issues that have haunted her throughout her entire life. We want to have a little chat with the teacher when we don't think a grade is correct. We want to intervene in girl drama and end the pain of exclusion, mean girls, and teasing. We want to pop the tires of the boy who broke our daughter's heart. It's unbelievable how a mother's heart works—it's a fierce love.

Sometimes our intervention is necessary, and we need to humbly ask God every morning to light our path and give us wisdom. But other times the intervention is our own doing, not God's will. To quote Brad McCoy, the father of former University of Texas football player Colt McCoy, we need to "prepare our child for the path, not the path for our child." It is dangerous when we focus on the path more than the person because it causes us to raise young women who are unprepared for life's challenges. Although our hearts are good and our intentions are loving, we are doing our girls a disservice when we rob them of opportunities to grow and rise up on their own behalf.

The only way we can find relief and release from this strong desire to fix and control is to remember that we are useless compared to God. No one can protect our daughters like He can. No one knows the training and refinement they will need for the journey ahead, but He does. No one can be with our daughters all the time, from the womb to the Promised Land, except for our God. Our faith grows when we trust God with our girls. They are, after all, not ours. They are His. We are raising them for His glory. He knows what they need in order to develop into the women He created them to be. We have to know when to step in and when to step out of the way—and the only way to really know that is to listen to God's responses to our prayers. He speaks—through His Word, His people, and His divinely appointed lessons (aka our circumstances).

Be intentional this week about trusting God with your girl. Be obedient when He leads you in your parenting. Allow Him to contend with those who contend with her.

Daughter

> Contend, LORD, with those who contend with me...
>
> *Psalm 35:1*

When someone hurts our feelings, it can be pretty tempting to want to hurt them back. Revenge is a very powerful temptation, especially when someone has shown such little care for our own feelings. It makes us not want to care about theirs, doesn't it?

Feelings like anger and hurt are a sign that something is going on that is not okay. If we let our feelings take control of us, we can make choices we will later regret. If we take our feelings to God until we calm down, He will help us see what is behind the emotion and what we need to do about it.

Sometimes we don't need to do anything at all. And that's exactly what this verse is telling us. *Contend, Lord, with those who contend with me.* "Contend" can mean fight, so this verse means *Fight, Lord, with those who fight with me.* It's like saying, "Okay, God, you deal with this one. I can't make things right, but You can."

This is a great verse to memorize so that in moments of powerful feelings, we have a way to calm ourselves and connect with God. We can ask Him to deal with the people who bother us. God has specific lessons for us as we grow up, and He also has lessons for other people. Sometimes when we take matters into our own hands, we get in the way of the lesson God has in mind for the person who is hurting us. And God's lessons are always more powerful than anything we could come up with on our own.

Besides, when you speak that verse back to God, you learn a lesson about self-control and trust. You learn that you can feel your feelings without losing control of your words and actions. Learning how to handle our emotions makes us incredibly powerful, far more powerful than a person who reacts or explodes. When we channel our emotions back to God, He will handle everything for us. When we trust Him with outcomes, He will move mountains. After all, He promises He will never leave you or forsake you (Heb 13:5).

Is there a certain situation or person who makes you feel like fighting or reacting? Isn't it comforting to know that God will fight for you so you don't have to?

This week, memorize this verse and practice saying it in your head when you start to feel your frustration rise. Let God contend with those who contend with you.

Mother

**Those who look to him are radiant; their faces are
never covered with shame.**

Psalm 34:5

Ah, beauty, a subject with rich topography for any woman.
Sometimes beauty is our friend; sometimes it is our oppo-
nent. Sometimes we pay it no mind and it settles on us like
a butterfly; other times we chase it despite the fact that it
will always elude those who pursue it.

We have a history with beauty, whether we want to dig
there or not. Our history is framed by the way we grew up,
messages from our parents and siblings, experiences with
our peers, our boyfriends, and our husband. At times we
have regarded beauty differently than others, and perhaps
it has caused us to regard ourselves differently as a result.

Our culture offers so many messages about beauty, but
the main one is to chase it down. There has to be a maga-
zine for it, a cream for it, an exercise regime for it, a diet
for it, or a surgery to make it happen. We are told by the
media, "Don't give up, and by all means, don't get old." It's
one thing to face the bombardment of these messages on

our own terms, but it becomes vastly different when we are shepherding the next generation of women, our daughters.

How do you want it to be different for your daughter? What things have you learned (perhaps the hard way) about what it means to be beautiful? What kind of messages do you speak to your daughter about beauty? And perhaps more important, what are your unspoken messages conveyed by the way you live and the way you treat yourself? I have taken some really foolish paths in my pursuit of beauty, but now I prioritize two: put on a smile and sunscreen.

God tells us something different about beauty. Instead of looking in the mirror, He tells us to *look to Him*. What a thought. When we look to Him instead of striving for that which we already possess, we are radiant. Radiance is an even higher, purer form of beauty—it glows from within.

This week consider your history with beauty—journal about it if you need greater clarity. What messages have been passed down to you? What do you want to pass along to your daughter and granddaughter? And what legacy do you want to stop in its tracks? With God's help, you can make a great impact on your daughter's concept of beauty. But it begins with you. If you aren't healthy and whole in this regard, the time to change is now.

Daughter

Those who look to him are radiant; their faces are never covered with shame.

Psalm 34:5

Who or what defines beauty for you?

Is it the magazines you look through? The singers and actresses you admire? Is it the trends and opinions of your friends? Or the cute boy in your class?

In our world today, so many messages are being thrown at you about what it means to be beautiful. Messages in advertising and media want you to *do something* about being beautiful because they want you to *buy something*. The message is that you are not good enough the way you are—you need something else. You need to buy a product or an outfit. You need a certain haircut and certain brands of makeup. You need to look a certain way in your jeans, shorts, or bathing suit. You need to be smaller or taller. Your hair needs to be lighter or darker, curlier or straighter, longer or shorter, with bangs or without bangs. It's impossible to keep up and even more impossible to feel good about yourself if you take every one of these messages to heart.

Because, honey, these messages are not directed specifically at you. They are to *girls in general*.

But the message in Psalm 34:5 is written to you, directly to your heart. God wants you to know that the only way to look and truly feel beautiful is by looking to Him. Feeling beautiful is most important because girls who feel beautiful are confident, fun, and free. They aren't worried about what other people are thinking because they already feel good the way they are. God created you, and He knows the most beautiful things about you. When you stay closely connected to Him, He draws out the most beautiful things about you, from the inside to the outside. And that is how you shine.

Try it this week. When you are tempted to think something negative about yourself or your beauty, remember Psalm 34:5. Look to God instead of the mirror. Do the things you love to do, and see if you don't feel more beautiful. Notice the effect that has on you and the people around you. Those who chase beauty never find it.

But those who look to God are radiant.

Mother

> **Daughters of Jerusalem, I charge you...Do not arouse or awaken love until it so desires.**
>
> *Song of Songs 2:7*

This topic is so big I sit here with a blank page and a humble prayer for wisdom with my pen.

Purity. Innocence. The body is God's temple. If only I could say that I have always lived this way, then I might have some wisdom from experience. But my experiences serve mostly to remind me of my lack of wisdom and my deep need for God and His grace. I had a chance for a do-over when my marriage ended, an opportunity to make different choices and try things God's way. When my girls are old enough, I will tell them exactly why and how things were different. Purity is not some old-fashioned notion from the ancient days, nor is it some all-or-nothing mindset that, once tainted, is hopeless and tossed aside. Purity is an ongoing process of decision making that involves going to God first about everything rather than pleasing the immediate gratification drive of self. Purity is about what we choose to read, listen to, and look at; what kind of conversations we have; what kind of messages we convey to our daughters about love, sex, dating, and marriage. It's about respecting what is holy in a world with an extreme deficit of reverence.

I want my girls to seek God's best in their lives. I want them to long for God's plan instead of pressing ahead with their own. And I want them to recognize real love when it finds them, instead of being confused by too much exposure to counterfeits. I want purity to be more than a mandate, a status, or a measure for "earning" God's love. I want to teach and model grace in a refreshing way, a way that invites rather than incites. I want them to know that *pleasing God is a pleasure*. I want them to eventually find lasting love with a man who sees them as God does—mind, body, spirit, and soul.

A mentor of mine explained purity to his daughters with this example. He took a piece of Scotch tape and explained that real love is meant to stick. He put it on a paper and held up the paper—yep, it stays put. But what happens when we put our love here, and here, and here? He stuck the tape to the wall, the sofa, and the table. Then he put that piece of tape on the paper and it fell to the ground. When it mattered, the love didn't stick. We have to be careful with our love. We have to guard our hearts, the wellspring of life (Prv 4:23).

This week, think about ways to encourage conversation about purity, not just as a sexual standard but also as a way of clean living all around. We are supposed to be a source of support and love, not of judgment and condemnation. Making good choices is not about pleasing (or appeasing) parents; it's about pleasing God. The sooner we shift to that truth, the better our relationship will be with our girls.

Daughter

**Daughters of Jerusalem, I charge you...Do not
arouse or awaken love until it so desires.**
Song of Songs 2:7

We were created to love and be loved. This is an essential part of the human design, made in the image of God, the Father of love. The feelings you have about being loved, needed, chosen, and adored are all beautiful things. But it's what we do with those feelings that can either bring us closer to God or lead us farther away.

The Bible tells us to guard our heart because it is the wellspring of life (Prv 4:23). This does not mean to shut it down or seal it off, but to be careful and thoughtful about when we share it, and with whom. The same goes for our bodies, which are the temple of the Holy Spirit (1 Cor 6:19). We have to be careful about sharing our temple. This can mean all kinds of things: the choices we make about what we allow to enter the temple of our minds on television or YouTube, what we wear, which friends we hang out with, and eventually the people we choose to date. This verse above reminds us not to be in such a rush to grow up. There is no hurry, and there is plenty to learn along the way.

Obeying God does not mean being all serious and having no fun. Obeying God means making choices that lead to your freedom, and being free is fun. It's fun to go through your day without worries, without fear of what people are thinking about you, or fear that you will be used or your heart will be broken. If you ask God to keep your heart and your body safe and pure, He will help you because He wants the very best for you. He wants you to experience real love at the right time. And in the meantime, He wants you to have freedom and fun, to enjoy your youth and look forward to an adult life that is full of options, hope, and promise.

There is no rush, sweet girl.

Everything will unfold for you at the right time, if you stay close to God.

Here is a prayer for you this week:

Dear Lord, help me to make good choices for my heart, my body, my spirit, and my mind. Thank You for loving me so much that You want the best for me. The world tells me to rush, but You tell me to take my time growing up. I have lots to learn and You have lots to teach me. Guard my heart and my temple as we go. In Jesus' name I pray, amen.

Mother

Therefore confess your sins to each other and pray for each other so that you may be healed. The prayer of a righteous person is powerful and effective.

James 5:16

Things that flourish in darkness cannot survive the glare of the light.

Sin is one of those things.

When we hide our sin, rationalize it, put up false fronts, and pretend that our thoughts, intentions, actions, and words are pure, we are giving sin the perfect cover of darkness to breed and multiply. Our sin grows and begins to take over other, formerly healthy areas of our existence. Like an undiagnosed and untreated cancer, sin is malignant and malicious. It will stop at nothing to take over more and more of your life.

But when we confess our sins, we yank their roots out of the darkness and place them in the light of God's holy presence, where they have no alternative but to wilt, shrivel, and die. The power of sin lies in its deception, in the hiding. Truth is the only effective antidote. It's good to bring our sins before God. It's good to bring our sins before our priest or pastor. It's also excellent practice to confess our sins to our inner, intimate circle of believing friends, the ones who hold us accountable because they are involved in our lives every day. When we bring our sins to God in the company of our trusted confidantes, we are well on the road to healing and freedom from the bondage of sin.

Our daughters need to know how to recover from sin. They need to see us walking out our faith in terms of actively turning from sin and deception and seeking the truth. They need to see us experience our own liberation so they will be less ashamed and intimidated to bring their own sins into the light. When our daughters share their sins with us, it is imperative that we remain steady and listen. Revealing shock or anger will only ensure that they will never choose us as a confidante again.

We need to unmask and demystify sin, calling it what it is. The more often we do this with our girls, the more comfortable they will become in dealing with sin swiftly and effectively themselves. This week, share an example of your own sin and seek forgiveness with your daughter. Perhaps you recently said something harsh or handled something in a way you regret? Go through the process of confession and repentance with her. Show her how it's done and how good it feels to be free and clear.

Daughter

> **Therefore confess your sins to each other and pray for each other so that you may be healed. The prayer of a righteous person is powerful and effective.**
>
> *James 5:16*

When we do something sinful, we can feel it in many ways. Sometimes we feel sick to our stomach or have trouble sleeping. Sometimes we can't stop thinking about our sin, wishing we could go back and do it differently or stressing and hoping we don't get caught. These bad feelings are called conviction, and even though conviction feels bad, it is actually good. It is a gift of the Holy Spirit to erase some of the false "good" feeling that surrounds sin. As a believer, it is impossible to ignore conviction forever.

Sin makes us feel shame. And shame makes us want to hide—maybe even want to pull away from God and other people. Sin thrives in darkness; only there can it grow. The more we hide our sin in the dark, the more it spreads and grows and infects other parts of our life. Sin steals our joy. Sin makes us unhealthy. Sin wants to drag us into the dark with it. Just like scary movies, where bad things only happen at night, sin can scare us only when we leave it in the dark. When we expose our sin to the light of truth, it can no longer grow!

We do this by confession. Confession can involve sharing our sins with God, our priest or pastor, our parent, or a trusted friend who will pray with us. The minute we take the load of sin off our shoulders by being truthful, we feel immediate relief, followed by peace and freedom. The reason sin is so awful and uncomfortable is because we are not meant to hide it and carry it around.

Jesus died for us so that we would not have to live like that! Let's show our gratitude for His gift by enjoying it.

Do you have any sins right now that you are tired of hiding? Something that you did or said that you feel terrible about and wish you could erase? Confess whatever is bothering you to God and ask for forgiveness. Apologize to someone if you believe you may have hurt them. Put your sin in the light and watch it shrivel up and go away.

Mother

> **We have different gifts, according to the grace given to each of us…**
>
> *Romans 12:6*

The waiter brings your meal out, and you really want what your friend is having. Your friend's husband is thoughtful and engaging, and your husband is distant and always on the phone. Other people's children are sweet, and yours fight and complain. When things like this happen, we are reminded that coveting is very much a part of human nature. If we aren't in a good place, it's easy to slide into the tendency of wanting that which we do not have.

But guess what? No one has a perfect life. Even people living a Cinderella story can really be lonely and unfulfilled. A woman with a great career might be pining for her children. A stay-at-home mom might be pining for her old office. A single woman might dream of a husband, while a married woman can't wait for hers to go out of town. A regular girl might dream of fame, while a famous one might dream of being anonymous. A curvy woman may be on a diet; a scrawny one may be saving up for fake curves. Blondes may get lowlights and brunettes may get highlights. We are often impossible to satisfy.

We do the same thing when we compare spiritual gifts. Someone who can preach might wish she were able to teach. Someone with a gift for ministering to youth might wish she had a great voice in order to sing and lead worship. At some point we have to understand and accept that true fulfillment has more to do with wanting what we have rather than having what we want, as the Sheryl Crow song says. When we have a grateful spirit, we can be happy for other women's successes without measuring ours against them. We can appreciate other people's gifts rather than coveting them when we are busy enjoying our own. Being content does not imply being complacent, but it does signify the maturity to recognize that everyone has different blessings.

This verse is a good one to memorize and tuck away so that when we are tempted to compare and complain, we can correct ourselves. And when our daughters need help and correction, we can be there, strong in our own gratitude and sense of purpose, to help them. If we let a covetous spirit go unchecked in our girls, it spawns a terrible root of envy, jealousy, mean girls, and unholy rivalry. The only way to foster true community for our girls is to lead by example.

How healthy are your friendships? Can you fully enjoy each other's gifts? Can you appreciate that which sparkles in their lives without your light growing dim? Our God is so generous. If we are rightly related to Him, the more we pour out, the more our cup refills. Let's teach our girls not to covet or hoard blessings.

Daughter

> **We have different gifts, according to the grace given to each of us...**
>
> *Romans 12:6*

It's hard not to compare ourselves to one another, isn't it? I remember being young and wishing that I looked like *her*, that I could play soccer like *her*, that I was as outgoing as *her*, that my hair looked like *hers*, and that he liked me instead of *her*. I liked other people's outfits, their abilities, and their lives. I was sure that it would probably be easier to be anyone else but me. I did the same thing with spiritual gifts, wishing that I were more confident when I taught Sunday school, or that I had a beautiful voice to sing in the choir.

It took me a long time to understand how this verse applied to me.

I don't want it to take that long for you or for my daughters. Once you understand the message of Romans 12:6, you can have a freedom that is usually understood only by women much older than you. It's available now—don't you want it? God gives us very specific gifts, spiritual and otherwise, from His grace to use for His glory.

It's impossible to see the gifts God has given you when you are busy looking at what He gave to everyone else. Meanwhile, the girls you might be jealous of are busy being jealous of someone else. Maybe even you. Isn't that silly? Everyone wants whatever they think they don't have. Tall girls wish they were shorter; short girls want to grow. Girls with wavy hair blow-dry their hair straight. Straight-haired girls curl it. A girl with only a few friends might wish to be more popular, and a popular girl may long for one deep friendship. One girl might long for a close family, while another girl wishes her family would just give her some space. An only child may be lonely, while a girl from a big family may dream of not having to share.

See? We have different gifts. But if we can get over paying so much attention to what other people have and what other people are doing, we can start to appreciate what we have right in front of us. We can start wanting what we have rather than putting so much focus on having what we want. This leads to peace, and peace leads to freedom—both of which lead to joy. How do we do this?

It's a simple shift I like to call *gratitude attitude*. When we shift our perspective to being thankful, we immediately are cured of wanting other people's blessings. We start to really want what God gave us and do more with what we have to work with. You have a role to fill, a big part to play in the Kingdom of God. The sooner you realize that, the more quickly you can get down to the business of figuring out what God wants you to do with what He gave you. And that, my dear, is the most exciting part about growing up.

This week, try a gratitude attitude. What special gifts did God give you, and what can you do with them?

Mother

> **Whoever loves discipline loves knowledge, but whoever hates correction is stupid.**
>
> *Proverbs 12:1*

Wow. I've always been against name-calling, but I suppose if it's in the Bible we can handle it. God does not mince words.

Discipline is not fun. It's not fun to receive it, and it sure isn't fun to be the one to dish it out. I'd much rather have fun and enjoy my kids than be the disciplinarian, but without the discipline, my kids ultimately wouldn't grow to be much fun. It's good for our girls to know that although we are authority figures in their lives, we are not the ultimate authority. We can't just call the shots either; we have to listen to and obey God.

There are seasons of discipline in our own lives that are difficult to endure. The consequences of poor choices yield a season of correction. But if we accept that season with humility and a desire to grow, we can get through it so much more gracefully. Other seasons are just plain hard, without any explanation at all. Perhaps at these times God is refining us for what only He knows lies ahead. He is making us stronger, wiser, and more diligent. He has bigger plans for us and wants us to be ready.

Correction, when done in love, is always for our growth. Even when it's hard to hear, we have to be brave enough to listen. We are going to make mistakes, but a mistake is never a failure if we learn from it and change our life accordingly. Rationalizing the feedback or correction we receive, finding fault in the messenger or the delivery of the message, or getting defensive all serve merely to deflect or delay God's good intention, *which is to help us grow.*

Listen when people have a message for you about your work, your parenting, your marriage, your relationships, your communication, and your talents. Try to hear what God is trying to tell you no matter how tempting it is to react to the discomfort of the moment. You are stronger than that. No discomfort equals no growth. Be willing to be temporarily uncomfortable so that God can have His way with you. Accept His discipline with the spirit of a woman who appreciates a challenge.

This week, instead of Why me? *think,* God, what do You want me to learn right now? *A humble student accepts a test.*

Daughter

> **Whoever loves discipline loves knowledge, but whoever hates correction is stupid.**
>
> *Proverbs 12:1*

Nobody enjoys being disciplined. It's no fun to be called out by a teacher, a principal, a policeman, or a parent. It's embarrassing to be caught. It can be painful to accept the consequences of our not-so-great decisions, especially when the consequences come from God, who can change our circumstances to reflect our choices—good or bad. Regardless of who else knows, He always knows. He is our ultimate authority.

God corrects us because He loves us. He wants to train us for the life He has prepared for us. That's why someone who loves knowledge also loves discipline. Because when you accept discipline, you always grow.

When someone corrects us, we may want to shut down, stop listening, pull away from that person, or come up with all kinds of excuses. We may not want to take responsibility for our mistakes—but we must. Resisting God when He is trying to help you change and grow is foolish. He will eventually teach you the lesson He aims to teach you—but you can make it take as long as you like, or it can be as uncomfortable as you want to make it. Our God is a patient God. He does not give up until we learn and change. It's okay to be uncomfortable. If we were always comfortable, we would never see or feel the need to change.

What are the messages God is sending you right now? Is He speaking through your parents, your teachers, your siblings, or your friends? Could it be that God is trying to teach you something or prepare you for something important? When God disciplines you, try to open your heart to really hear what is going on. God loves those He disciplines. Be flattered that the Creator of the Universe is paying attention to your growth and development. He is preparing you for your future.

Look for ways to get ready.

This week when you are corrected or disciplined, instead of getting angry or upset, try to look for the lesson. Remember that a chance to learn is a blessing, not a punishment. Thank God when He teaches you.

Mother

> **The words of the reckless pierce like swords, but the tongue of the wise brings healing.**
>
> *Proverbs 12:18*

Taming our tongues is a lifetime pursuit. Sometimes I feel like I have to chase mine down rodeo style, with a horse and a lasso. When we aren't being intentional and prayerful, our tongues take off without us, filterless and dangerous, wreaking havoc over all kinds of situations and relationships. Nothing can fill me with regret more quickly than replaying a situation and wishing I had just simply shut my mouth. It's hard to regret silence—unless you had the chance to say, "I love you," or "I'm sorry," and you didn't do it.

Daughters can push our buttons. They know us intimately, so they know exactly what sets us off. One adolescent hormone outburst can be enough to push us right over the edge. Our daughters' sarcasm or rudeness can awaken our own dragons, and the result can be an explosion of immaturity and hurtful words. It is precisely when we feel the potential to be most immature that God is calling upon our maturity. Someone has to be the lighthouse when the seas get heavy, and that someone is called Mom.

The words and tone we choose when speaking to our

girls can hurt them or heal them. Some of my adult friends are still dressing wounds or hiding scars created long ago by a comment made by their mother. Some friends are still trying to shake off old definitions and labels, likely affixed in a clueless or venomous moment. Some friends never feel thin enough, smart enough, pretty enough, or good enough for any blessing or compliment they receive today. The whispers of old comments still sting and hold them back. We have to remember that God alone has the power to define. We have no business limiting our girls with our own perspectives. Any broken area of our own lives or our own legacies that goes unhealed is a potential injury we might pass along.

When we start tending to our hearts and choosing kind words when we speak to ourselves, this outpouring will be like living water to those around us. Kindness begets kindness. You know the saying "Hurt people hurt people." Well, guess what—the inverse is also true. Healed people heal people. And loved people love people.

Our hearts influence our minds, and our minds direct our words and actions. We have to go deep to have the kind of transformation that overhauls our communication. This week, think of the legacy you want to leave. Hurt or heal? Choose your words wisely.

Daughter

The words of the reckless pierce like swords, but the tongue of the wise brings healing.

Proverbs 12:18

Carelessly chosen words can cause damage that is impossible to undo. Hurtful things we say in a moment of pain or anger can often do more damage than we ever meant to do. When we are upset, we are not thinking clearly. We are reckless.

It takes a lifetime to learn how to tame our tongue. But the first step is to learn when we need some space to cool off. Even a few minutes of separation from a heated situation can allow room for the Holy Spirit to come in and save us from being unkind.

Our words have the power to hurt—and to heal. We can choose the effect we want to have. You can see this happen in a group when girls start talking and the conversation turns to someone else and becomes gossip. The more everyone contributes, the uglier it can get. But if one person, just one, has the courage to change the subject, say something nice, or say something funny, the whole tone and direction of the conversation can shift. This is an example of the tongue of the wise bringing healing—an uncomfortable conversation can be saved by one brave person who uses her gifts of speaking truth or humor to get the group back on track. If we do nothing in the face of reckless words, we are not living our faith. Even if we aren't the one speaking recklessly, we are condoning the decision with our silence or our laughter.

I have adult friends who are still hurt by comments made during their childhood. Our words can wound deeply, and that damage can last a long time. We have no business defining anyone with our words. Only God has the power to define us or anyone else. We have to be responsible for our own tongues.

Take time this week to think before you speak. Use the power of your words to shift conversations that have gone in an unkind direction. Say something nice to someone else and watch how that blessing passes on. If you are going to make a difference with your speech, make a difference for good... for God's glory.

Mother

> "Glory to God in the highest heaven, and on earth peace to those on whom his favor rests."
>
> *Luke 2:14*

Glory is an interesting phenomenon in our culture; most people seek it for themselves. We want to be recognized. We want to get credit, to go first, to be seen, and to win. We want the promotion and the publicity. We want acknowledgment for our hard work and the accolades of our peers. Society teaches us that our own personal glory is a sign of success. But God teaches us a different lesson about glory, real glory. It all belongs to Him. Everything He has taught us and given us as both challenge and blessing (these things eventually become synonymous) is to be poured back out as an offering to Him, to reflect the light back toward Him. We are to turn the credit and the power back to the source—glory to God in the highest.

One of my daughters, Isabelle, is an exceptional runner. I love to run, but this girl has a gift from God. She gets very nervous before races, often taking it out on me by being short and snippy. I understand. One day before a race she was very stressed and finally admitted to me that she was really nervous. She asked me what she could do about that.

"It depends," I said.

"Depends on what?" she asked.

"On the glory," I said.

"Whose glory?" Isabelle looked at me, confused.

"Exactly." I explained, "That's the point. If you are racing for your glory, you should be nervous. Some days you will have a great race and you will be on top of the world. Other days you will have a bad race and you will sink into despair. But if you are racing for God's glory, that's something different all together. If you are using your gift to glorify God, you can just go out there and give what you've got and have fun every time. You can enjoy the gift He gave you, and you will always feel satisfied because it's no longer just about you. It's way bigger."

She got this relieved look on her face. "That," she said. "That's what I want. His glory."

"Great," I said. "Know it or not, you just changed your life."

We headed off to the track and she had a great race, free from all of her self-imposed pressure and anxiety about measuring up to some constantly changing bar she sets for herself, comparing herself ruthlessly to other runners or to her previous finish times. She ran for God. I hope she always does.

How can you help your daughter see that her gifts are for God's glory, not her own? How can you teach her the freedom that comes when we cease being self-seeking? How can you live that lesson by reflecting your own light back to the Source, crediting God for all He has given you?

Daughter

> "Glory to God in the highest heaven, and on earth peace to those on whom his favor rests."
>
> *Luke 2:14*

The message from the world tells us that we should seek glory for ourselves. We should strive to win, to be first, to be the best, to get all the credit, to be recognized, to shine.

God tells us something different than the world tells us. He tells us that glory belongs to Him alone. And that when we use the gifts He has given us, we should use them in such a way that the glory is reflected back on Him. How do we do this? Well, we try our best with what He has given us to work with, in school, in sports or other activities, and in all our relationships. We offer our best because He has given His best for us.

Additionally, we are grateful. When we do well and there is an opportunity to take credit, we share the credit with Him and with others who helped us. Maybe you have seen athletes do this on television after they win a big game or an Olympic medal? They are interviewed and they use their chance in front of the world to thank God for giving them a gift. Or maybe an actress wins an award for a great performance and she gets to give an acceptance speech. You can always tell the people of faith because they are the ones who give the credit back to God. Instead of hogging their moment in the spotlight, they shine the light back to the Source, which is God.

These are big examples, Olympic medals and Oscar wins, but there are countless ways to give glory to God every single day. And you don't have to be on television to make a big impact on the world by returning the glory to God. Seeking glory for God instead of yourself frees you from unnecessary pressure and anxiety. You don't have to be someone who lives under huge pressure to perform—grades, sports, extracurricular activities—because if you are simply using your gifts to glorify God, you are already a success. You can actually enjoy the gifts and talents you have been given, which is what God truly intended. Your gifts are not supposed to feel like a burden! When we strive to put ourselves first all the time, we are constantly struggling and comparing ourselves to others or to our own previous efforts. It becomes harder and harder to be satisfied, and we are always wondering if we could have done better. Release yourself from a life like that.

This week, find ways to give glory to God, not to yourself. You will be surprised by how much more enjoyable it is to do the things you love. You may even be surprised by how much better you do these things when you are doing them for someone besides yourself. Glory to God means peace for you.

Mother

> **Join with me in suffering, like a good soldier of Christ Jesus. No one serving as a soldier gets entangled in civilian affairs, but rather tries to please his commanding officer.**
>
> *2 Timothy 2:3–4*

It's easy to get mired down by the opinions of others, the notion of pleasing others, and the snare of gossip. For believers, these things are all merely civilian affairs. We have a higher post and a higher calling, and we have a far greater commanding officer to obey and please.

I have gotten stuck so many times trying to be a pleasing wife, a pleasing daughter, a pleasing friend, a pleasing employee, and a pleasing parent. Every time I am in a place like this, I can feel myself constantly shifting, as if the wind blows me in all directions and the waves toss me this way and that. I have no steady compass because I have taken my eyes off God. When I break my gaze on God, I lose sight of what is real and lasting in my life. The voices of others start to take on increasing and inappropriate levels of volume and importance. I find myself scrambling to get things done, but I'm not really sure that the things I'm doing are what I'm really supposed to be doing. My sense of purpose and satisfaction has dimmed.

This voice speaks to me and snaps me to attention, just like a soldier. I can hear God chiding me, *"Kristin, these are civilian affairs that you are so concerned with. Let them go. Turn back to me. I have everything under control. You do not."* What a relief. I am not in charge of what other people think. I cannot control my children. It is impossible to be authentic and pleasing at the same time, all the time. All I really have to be is myself. All I really have to do is obey God's call on my life, my time, my talents. He is my commanding officer, and my life's work is designed to bring Him glory and be pleasing to Him.

If I can live my life this way, I can model this kind of peaceful and purposeful living for my daughters. I can lead them by example. I can demonstrate how I turn from gossip and how I disengage from the constant temptation to please others. I can only hope to raise girls who turn to God first if I myself am turning to Him first. If our words and our choices do not match, our teaching is ultimately void.

Be scrupulous this week in your examination of your desire to please. If you are out of balance, figure out how you are going to reset the scales in your life. Pleasing God is the first order of operations, every day. Break free of being consumed with civilian affairs, and untether yourself from the trivial. Straighten your shoulders and assume the stance of a soldier—then act like one.

Daughter

> **Join with me in suffering, like a good soldier of Christ Jesus. No one serving as a soldier gets entangled in civilian affairs, but rather tries to please his commanding officer.**
>
> *2 Timothy 2:3–4*

Maybe you are wondering, *What exactly are civilian affairs?*

In the military, civilian affairs are trivial things that are going on between people that have nothing to do with the mission or the assignment of the soldiers. To regular people like us, civilian affairs might be gossip, who likes whom, who is wearing what, where people are going, who got in trouble, who did well, and who didn't. Civilian affairs are meaningless details in comparison to our larger mission.

That mission is pleasing God.

It's easy to be distracted by our desire to please everyone besides God. Our teachers, our coaches, our parents, our youth leaders, our friends, and our peers all have very strong influences in our life. Some of this desire to please is a healthy and good response to authority figures that God has placed in our lives. But when we go too far with this desire to please, so far that we have a hard time hearing God's voice because all the other voices have grown too loud, we have entered a place that is spiritually unhealthy. God wants to come first; He makes this abundantly clear in Scripture, over and over. And He will make it clear in life lessons as well. When we put Him first and respect His will, we are peaceful. Things flow. When we start to put everything else before Him, things do not flow. They start to get increasingly difficult.

This verse is a great one to memorize and have tucked away for those moments when we are tempted to put the world first. I use it myself when I start to feel anxiety about what everyone else is doing, or what everyone else is saying. I tell myself, *It's just civilian affairs,* and it calms me down and reminds me that no matter how stressed I might feel, this is not the big picture.

Like cards, I reshuffle the deck of my thoughts, and God turns up as King. I can rest, knowing that He is in control and in charge. I am simply one of His soldiers, on a mission for Him. It is a relief to remind myself that I am not in control. I am not expected to have all the answers or know what to do in every situation. I am not supposed to please everyone, or always be pleasing. I am expected to honor God as my commanding officer and take my assignments directly from Him.

Remember your mission, and this verse, this week.

Mother

Through patience a ruler can be persuaded, and a gentle tongue can break a bone.

Proverbs 25:15

Sometimes when I have an important message to convey to my kids or a crucial moment when I need to discipline them, I blow it. Whenever I try to have a meaningful conversation while in an emotional state, it backfires, usually right back in my face. Impactful parenting is intentional and calm. A patient demeanor and gentle language defuse a highly charged situation and restore peace. Peace sets the backdrop for teachable moments.

A soft and gentle spirit has far greater strength than we might expect. People who are always flying off the handle are not strong, despite their bluster and bravado. People like this are unsafe and unreliable…and often what they have to say is disregarded simply because they are always in a worked-up state. Like the adult characters in Peanuts cartoons, their voices become a monotone drone. Too much volatility and volume yield less effect, not more. Real strength comes from being able to control one's emotions, responding rather than reacting.

How do we cultivate a gentle spirit in the midst of real life? Real life is often riddled with unanticipated challenges, button pushing, and legitimate frustration. My friend Dawn often reminds me to "make space for grace." I hear her voice in my head often when my emotions threaten to get the best of me, making the worst of me. I remember I need to take a few minutes away with God. If I can physically remove myself, it's even better. For example, stepping into another room, going out on the patio, or running a bath. If I can take a few moments to breathe and invite God into the situation, I can be restored to clear thinking. My peace and patience return, sufficient to see things through to resolution. If I don't have the luxury of physical space, I can create some spiritual space by turning inward for a moment, breathing, and inviting God in. A whispered prayer on my lips is far better than other things I could mutter in a moment of exasperation, that's for sure. And as an added bonus to my calm is the visual example my children see when I take my irritation to God instead of taking it out on them. They are beginning to understand that sometimes Mom just needs some space, and it encourages them to do likewise.

If we can take the time we need to get right with God, we will ultimately do right by the people we love. Patience and gentleness may not be our default setting, but we can change and we can cultivate these traits in our hearts with God's help.

This week, when you feel frustration mount, try to make space for grace and see what happens. Invite God into your chaos and watch Him work.

Daughter

> **Through patience a ruler can be persuaded, and a gentle tongue can break a bone.**
>
> *Proverbs 25:15*

Are there moments when there is something you really want from your mom? Maybe there is something she simply does not, or will not, understand no matter how hard you try to explain? Does it seem sometimes like she just doesn't get it?

It's easy to get frustrated in these moments when emotions are high. When we get frustrated, we naturally get impatient, and then what started as a difficult situation goes quickly from difficult to impossible. When this occurs, no matter whom the conflict is with, we run the risk of hurting the relationship with our words. Our words can do far deeper and greater damage than we would ever intend. That is why God encourages us to be patient and have a gentle tongue (meaning to choose our words carefully and thoughtfully).

This happens regularly with our moms. We have different opinions on a subject, we both start explaining our sides, tempers flare, each gets frustrated with the other, voices rise, and eventually there could be an explosion.

Maybe you get sent to your room, or she goes to hide in hers. Nothing gets resolved this way. The end result is separation, not solution.

A patient, gentle approach with your mother will always work better. When we don't let the situation get too emotional, we can stick with the facts and come to a logical conclusion together, possibly even a compromise. Patience shows maturity, which can sometimes cause a parent to adjust a no to a maybe. When you fly off the handle at your mom, this only confirms that you are not ready to do or have the thing you think you need.

Patient people are powerful people. If you can get control over your emotions at a young age, you will have a far more peaceful life. When you are able to think clearly and speak gently, people will want to listen to your perspective and take your opinions into consideration.

This week pay attention to the warning signs when you are about to lose your cool. Notice how your body feels, how your spirit feels, and what's going on in your head and in your heart. If you can feel your frustration rise, pause and ask God to come into the moment right now. This is called making a space for grace.

Mother

In the same way, let your light shine before others, that they may see your good deeds and glorify your Father in heaven.

Matthew 5:16

So many women spend their lives with their light shrouded.

We begin, in the innocence of our youth, with so many plans, so many big ideas, so much passion. And if we aren't careful, time and responsibilities can steal our shine. We begin to do and live for the people we love and forget the things that we were created to do and love. Our purpose gets hazy and muddled.

I know women who spend their lives caring for kids, running errands, doing chores, and biding time. Over time, the needs of their children diminish, but they are still carving their time the same way they did when their children needed full-time care. They start to wander through their days aimlessly, not really knowing what to do with themselves. And when their kids grow and leave, they wilt and wither and are totally lost. Their flailing makes me ache.

Our daughters need to know that we are more than moms. Even though mothering is a huge and important endeavor and our children are high priorities, being a mom cannot be the full sum of who we are. Our girls need to see the full spectrum of femininity, and the best and closest example is their mothers. Remember the things you love to do and start doing them. Resurrect your passions, interests, hobbies, and skills. Share them with your daughter.

Our light is not meant to be hidden. Imagine many years from now if your daughter were to read an old journal or see an old scrapbook of yours and have no idea that girl or woman was her mother! Imagine her confusion: *My mother liked to sing? Write? Run? Paint? Practice law? Speak French? Travel? Run a business? Surf? Ski? Hike? Ride horses? Really?*

Your identity should not be a surprise to your daughter. God created you to be you, and He gave you a girl to guide into womanhood. Show her what a woman is all about.

Your assignment this week is to find an old journal or start a new one. Start asking some questions and digging through your rubble. Clear the dust. Ask God to help you let your light shine. How else will you illuminate the path for your daughter?

Daughter

In the same way, let your light shine before others, that they may see your good deeds and glorify your Father in heaven.

Matthew 5:16

God created you to shine, for His glory.

He did not create you to hide, to slouch, or to reduce yourself in any way. He created you to be *you*, in the fullest.

When you are comfortable and confident, it makes everyone around you feel at home. Letting your light shine is not the same thing as hogging the spotlight. A spotlight comes from another source and is intended to focus the attention on the star. Letting your light shine refers to the light coming from within you, which is meant to focus the attention and the glory on God. When we use the gifts He gave us with happiness and humility, we give God pleasure. He wants to see His children enjoying His gifts.

Think about the things you love to do—I mean *really* love to do. God created you to love and be good at specific things. When you do them, how do you feel? I bet you feel happy and free. Some girls may feel slightly shy or embarrassed because they do not like to be noticed when they do their thing. Any attention at all might make them want to hide their light. Don't be tempted to slip into the shadows. Because when you are enjoying your gifts, you share that joy with others. Your gifts from God turn into gifts you give away, and the way you have been blessed becomes a blessing.

The real source of your light, what really makes you shine, is your faith in God. This is what the Bible means in this verse: Don't hide your faith. Don't stuff your talents in a drawer. Use what God has given you to the fullest of your ability. And when people compliment you, direct the attention back to God. Then you will always be humble and your energy will always be refreshed to do more good things.

Do you know what your gifts are? A good clue is to think about the things you really love to do! This week, notice if you are tempted to hide your talents or your true self. Do you try to minimize your gifts? Do you ever hide your light? Think about opportunities you have where you can let your light shine.

Turn the spotlight onto the real star—our Almighty God!

Mother

> You have persevered and have endured hardships
> for my name, and have not grown weary.
>
> *Revelation 2:3*

I recently took my kids on a hike in the mountains in Southern California. Our route started off easy enough, a wide fire road with a relatively mild ascent. We had periodic shade to stop and drink water. As we approached our destination, called Inspiration Point, the going got much tougher. The ascent became so steep, rocky, and dusty that we started to wonder if we were going to make it to the top without skidding back, and if we got there, how were we going to get safely back down? Luke, my oldest, suggested we perhaps should turn back.

But we came for Inspiration Point. I didn't want to bail on our goal, but I also didn't want to do anything foolish to put my children at risk. I paused, looked up, and asked God what to do. I felt peace, so we continued our climb. We made it safely, and the view was amazing. I was so glad we did not turn back early; we were glad we persevered. In our immediate-gratification culture, it can be extra sweet to earn a pleasure. And the view from Inspiration Point is truly a pleasure.

That climb got me thinking. There are things in my life that are uncomfortable or uncertain to me, things I get close to attempting or completing, and a gust of fear makes me turn around. I want to be an example for my kids of someone who presses on and presses in and does not shrink back in the face of a challenge. I could talk about courage and perseverance in the context of their lives until I am blue in the face, but if I am not living it in mine, my words have no basis, no merit.

This week, think about the areas in your life where you get close to breaking through but turn back too soon. Why do you allow fear to hold you back in these areas? Think about ways you can press into your fears and manifest courage in your life. Talk about these things, your struggles and your victories, with your daughter. Perhaps your openness will solicit an open heart on her part, and you can have a conversation about the value of perseverance and overcoming fear. God is glorified by our willingness to endure.

Struggles yield strength. Be willing to push beyond your comfort zone in order to grow. Maybe you could use an adventure together?

Daughter

> **You have persevered and have endured hardships for my name, and have not grown weary.**
> *Revelation 2:3*

Perseverance and endurance are big words, maybe because they mean something big—the ability and the courage to keep going when things get tough. Characteristics like endurance and perseverance don't just come about naturally. They are not things that some people simply have and others just don't. Endurance and perseverance are built within us through challenging times.

We can live soft lives if we choose, always choosing comfort over a challenge. It's like watching an adventure show on television rather than actually going outside and having adventures of our own. The problem if we choose to live soft lives is that we, too, become soft. And then when hard times or real challenges come, we are too weak to handle them.

We can choose to improve our perseverance and endurance, even in ordinary times. We can choose to earn things rather than ask for them. We can stop looking for the easy way out and take the more challenging path. We can face our fears and be willing to be uncomfortable while we grow.

I have run marathons (which are a little more than

twenty-six miles) and even some ultramarathon distances (like fifty miles). I don't do it because I'm good at it (I'm okay, not great) or because running comes easily for me (it does not—it's hard!). I do it because I like to practice pushing my limits. I know that real-life tests will come—they always do—and when they come, I want to be as ready as possible. I want to know I can keep going when things get tough.

Take some time this week to think about areas where you might be living a soft life. How might this weaken you later? How can you take steps today to strengthen yourself?

How is God calling on you to keep going in your life, even if things seem difficult? Remember endurance is built step by step, so ask God to help you take some steps this week!

God is glorified when we seek Him to strengthen us.

Mother

> **Do you not know that your bodies are temples of the Holy Spirit, who is in you, whom you have received from God? You are not your own.**
>
> *1 Corinthians 6:19*

I have looked at my body in many ways: as a clothes rack, an object of beauty and vanity, an object of scorn and criticism, a sensual creation, an incubator of life, a sustainer of life, an athlete, and with the scrutiny of middle-aged eyes, noticing shifts and changes. When I first experienced real understanding of this verse, it was like seeing myself for the first time.

I suddenly felt acute shame for all the times I was critical of myself, all the times I compared myself to someone else, all the times I was dissatisfied or disapproving. I regretted decisions I made when I ate too much or too little, or indulged any of my desires in unhealthy ways. I mistakenly thought that my body was my gift for my own pleasure, under my own power, never really grasping the concept that my body is a shell, a housing unit for my soul, a temple of the Holy Spirit, who resides within me. I was too busy striving to take the time to consider the real intention behind my creation: the gift of my life.

I believe that having daughters also helped change the way I regard my own body. I want so much for them to have healthier views than I did and avoid some of the pitfalls and sidetracks where I got lost and wounded. I want them to have a sense of reverence for their temple and to treat it with respect and gratitude.

I share this verse with my daughters in the context of good and godly choices, things like nutrition, exercise, rest, hydration, attire, relationships, and sexuality. If you really believe your body is a temple, that it is not your own, you will make different choices. We have a responsibility to share this verse and also to live a life that manifests it. I read an article that said the best thing a mother can do to positively impact the body image of her daughter is to pay attention to the way she regards herself.

This week be aware and intentional about the way you speak of and to yourself and how you treat your temple. Watch the vocabulary you use—not just in conversation with your daughter, but with your friends, on your phone, or even in your head. Try to pay yourself a compliment in the vicinity of her ears, even if it feels awkward at first. If we don't love ourselves and treat ourselves respectfully, how on earth can we expect as much from our daughters?

Daughter

Do you not know that your bodies are temples of the Holy Spirit, who is in you, whom you have received from God? You are not your own.

1 Corinthians 6:19

Think of a time you borrowed something special from a close friend, something you knew she really cared about, and she was nice enough to let you use it. She trusted you to take care of it and expected that you would return it in the same good condition as when she lent it to you. How does this make you feel?

You were probably extra careful with it, maybe even more careful than you would have been if you were using your own. You wanted to live up to the level of trust that she gave you when she offered to share her special thing. It may have even felt like a relief to return it, knowing it was safely back to being her responsibility.

I have felt that way when a friend let me borrow a special dress or a piece of jewelry, or even trusted me to housesit or babysit their dog or child. I am on high alert, even more careful than normal.

This verse from 1 Corinthians explains that our body is not our own. Think about that for a second. Maybe you have always felt like you own the body you walk around in, that it is yours to treat however you please. Maybe you aren't always kind to your body. Maybe you don't always give it proper nutrition, hydration, rest, care, or respect. Your body belongs to God. It is a temple for the dwelling of His Holy Spirit, *who resides within you.* Just as you would treat a special item from your friend with extra care and protection, think about treating your body (which is on loan from God) in the same way.

This week, try thinking about your body as a temple, as something precious that does not belong to you but is on loan from God. He is trusting you to be careful. How does this impact the way you eat? What you drink? How you dress? Your exercise or activity level? The risks you might take? The words you use to talk to yourself or others? The way you see yourself?

Allow your new way of thinking to affect your actions and choices. Take good care of your temple.

Mother

> "Come to me, all you who are weary and burdened, and I will give you rest."
>
> *Matthew 11:28*

We have the weirdest notions about *busy* in our present culture, such as, the busier you are, the more important you are. Or having less time for yourself means you are more necessary to everyone else. We have snippets of conversation with friends and family and call that connection. We say we are "so busy," "just slammed," and "have no time." But we say it with a measure of pride instead of regret. We complain about our lack of time, but we don't make any changes to the way we live.

And we are doing the same thing with our kids, stacking their schedules to look like ours! We book school, sports, tutors, church, extracurricular activities, and community service, leaving little family or free time.

God designed us for balance. How do we know if we are trying to do too much? Well, the first answer is *we're exhausted*. If we are tired to the bone, it's a sign to stop what we're doing and get quiet and still. It's time to evaluate our priorities and get straight with God. Maybe we are doing too much? Or maybe we are simply spending time on the wrong things? When we are properly aligned, we are refreshed by what we do, not wrecked.

You are no good for anyone else if you have not taken care of yourself. Putting everyone else first and scrambling around in a frenzy does not make you a better mother; it just makes you a better martyr. Time with God comes first, then care of self, and then you are ready to do your part for others. Best of all, you will do what you are called to do with grace, presence, and intention. A legacy of busyness is not what you want to pass onto your daughter.

Notice this week if you are scattered or scrambling. How do you feel as you go about your daily life? Are you depleted and drained? If so, it's time to make some new choices. Rest is not a luxury; it is an ordained part of life, faith, self, and family.

Rushing just means you get nowhere sooner. Chill and be. Jesus says, "Come to me." What's stopping you?

Daughter

> "Come to me, all you who are weary and burdened, and I will give you rest."
>
> *Matthew 11:28*

It's possible you may not even remember a time when people weren't so busy all the time. Imagine that there was ever a time when a house had one phone number to share, no one had cell phones, or texting, and no one had an Internet connection. When you wanted to talk to someone, you called or stopped by. You might even try to call someone and get a busy signal, which just meant try again sometime later. People worked or studied during the week, but weekends were disconnected from the world, time to hang out with family and friends without activities or a schedule. Lounging on the sofa on Sunday afternoon wasn't lazy; it was normal. It was good. It was rest.

Today with cell phones and computers, people can be reached anytime. The workweek blurs into the weekend if Mom or Dad gets called into the office or has to answer email. Some teachers give weekend homework. Sports have weekend games. There is no longer a real weekend break. We are losing our sense of time and balance.

Do you often feel tired? Do you struggle to keep up with

all the demands on your time? School, sports, activities, tutors, social time . . . is it ever just too much? If you feel this way, there is a very good and real chance that you indeed are doing too much—more than God intended for good health and balance. If we are never quiet, and if we never make time to rest, we will never have time for a connection with God. And if we disconnect from God, we end up disconnected with ourselves. Taking time to rest is not a luxury of long ago. You need it today. God wants that for you.

This week, think about how you spend your free time. Do you have enough? If you feel out of balance, ask God to show you what to do. He may encourage you to do one less activity after school, or skip the sleepover or birthday party and relax at home, or turn off the screens and spend some time outside.

Start a conversation with your family one night at dinner and discuss ways you can reclaim free time and maybe some relaxing family time too.

Mother

> **Therefore, although in Christ I could be bold and order you to do what you ought to do, yet I prefer to appeal to you on the basis of love...**
>
> *Philemon 1:8–9*

I sat in a parenting class once and the instructor said, "There are no rules without relationship." Well, there may be rules, but perhaps none that are actually enforceable without relationship. Let's be honest, once our kids are no longer infants that we can strap into car seats and strollers, they have minds and wills of their own. We can make rules and mandates, and attempt to enforce compliance through force or punishment, but at some point the effect of all that simply wears thin, then wears off entirely.

Kids can fake obedience, say the words we want to hear, and do the right thing when we are watching, but have a completely different life when we aren't around. Eventually, with teenagers, our punitive stances lose their oomph, and kids simply start to shut down and not care. They can grow bigger, stronger, and smarter than we are. No matter what we want to believe, we are not in control; they are their own people. By virtue of giving birth, we were never promised a lifetime of compliance in return. We weren't even promised relationship. We have to do our part to earn that over time.

God, in all His unfathomable wisdom, has known this about human nature from the dawn of ages—ordering someone to do something does not yield obedience; it yields compliance. That is precisely why Jesus invites us to faith instead of forcing it. He wants relationship with us. He wants our obedience to spring forth from love, or not at all. If obedience doesn't come from love, from relationship, *it isn't real*.

The sooner we understand this about our children, the better. Every time we get into a tricky or treacherous parenting situation, we would do well to pause, pray, reset, breathe, and return to relationship first. From an authoritarian basis of frustration or anger, all we end up doing is alienating our girls at the precise moment we need them to listen! From a basis of love, we can communicate with our daughters. In an environment of mutual respect, our opinions are exchanged and have value. They will be more inclined to heed our words because they have been spoken in love. We cannot impose our values or our ways of thinking on our girls—but by loving them, we can make them want to listen.

This week, take the opportunity to do this one thing differently: in a moment of frustration, stop. *Take the time you need to cool off, then approach your daughter again when you are calm. Sit down when you talk; don't stand over her. Speak from your heart and ask for a chance to start over.*

Daughter

Therefore, although in Christ I could be bold and order you to do what you ought to do, yet I prefer to appeal to you on the basis of love...

Philemon 1:8–9

God is the Father of the Universe; everything is under His control. He could easily force us to obey Him in every way, and yet He gives us free will. We can make our own decisions, good or bad.

Why do you suppose someone as powerful as God lets His people go in all directions?

God knows that forcing you to obey is not the same as obedience that comes from a loving relationship. And that is what God desires to have with you. God wants to draw you close to Him; He wants to share His heart and His goodness with you. He wants you to experience His unconditional love so that you know to the core of your heart that He adores you just as you are, no matter what you do. It takes some people a lifetime to really understand and absorb that fact, and, sadly, some people never understand it at all.

Once you understand that you are unconditionally loved, you are open and ready to be taught. God shares His laws and standards with us in His Word, and we begin to see, through the trial and error of our own choices, that His ways are best because He wants what's best for us. Truly. When we experience the outcome of our bad choices, we begin to appreciate His teaching even more and want to do things His way. As our relationship deepens over time, so does our trust. Over time, we learn to go to Him first. This is what He was after all along.

God appeals to you on the basis of love, not force. You are free to choose in the hopes that you will choose Him because choosing Him really is choosing love. His rules and laws are not in place to try and suffocate you or limit you—they are intended to set you free.

Good relationships are like this. They do not make demands without a foundation of respect and understanding. They are not one way, all giving or all taking. They are founded in love and respect. Good relationships take time to build.

This week, think about the time you devote to your relationship with God. Is the time you offer enough to yield a deep and lasting connection? Think about ways you can create more time and space with God.

Mother

> "In your anger do not sin": Do not let the sun go down while you are still angry, and do not give the devil a foothold.
>
> *Ephesians 4:26–27*

Many women were raised with the mistaken notion that there is something inherently *wrong* with anger, that if you are feeling angry, it points to something wrong with you. Many women were taught as girls that anger is unladylike and should be stuffed away and snuffed out at all costs.

I am of the belief, after enough therapy and spiritual growth, that emotions shouldn't necessarily be labeled good or bad—they simply are. However it's what we do with them that can alter them in positive or negative ways. For example, jealousy can be considered an ugly emotion—but instead of acting on it in an immature or unhealthy way, if we sit with it long enough, it can reveal some things deep within us that need healing. It points us back to God. This can make it a good thing.

It's the same thing with anger. If we have no self-control and we let our unchecked rage fly with little concern for the ramifications of our words and actions, our anger can be a scary thing (especially to those we love). But if we can step back from our anger just far enough to get some air and some perspective, we can see that anger is often a sign that points to an important issue or area of trouble.

The more confident and peaceful we are in managing our own anger, the less fear and resentment we will have toward our daughters' anger. We will not encourage them to fear it or stuff it away because we are comfortable in handling our own. We will see an angry outburst as an opportunity to teach something of timeless value to our girls: Take the necessary time to cool off, of course, but try to heed God's warning when possible and make peace before bed. Sleepless, restless nights can give the enemy a foothold, allowing him to speak more lies and confusion into an already muddled situation. Even if it isn't wise or possible to go as deep as necessary in conversation, at least find a way to reconnect and soothe before sleeping.

God's mercies are always fresh in the morning, and you will be too.

This week, work on pausing in an angry or frustrating moment. Attempt to intellectualize your emotion and encourage your brain to work in tandem with the indignation of your heart, not against it or in spite of it. Use your power for good, like a generator. Ask the Holy Spirit to enlighten you to areas of growth and healing.

Daughter

> "In your anger do not sin": Do not let the sun go down while you are still angry, and do not give the devil a foothold.
>
> *Ephesians 4:26–27*

Do you label certain emotions as "good" and others as "bad"? For example, good emotions are things like happiness, peace, and joy, and bad emotions are anger, jealousy, and sadness. What if you erased that way of thinking and made all emotions equal, without any label of good or bad? What if every emotion was simply an arrow that pointed you to a deeper connection with God and a deeper understanding of yourself?

Anger gets a bad rap, doesn't it? From the time we are little kids we are told not to get angry, or to stuff our anger away and just deal with it or get along. But did you know that even Jesus got angry? Yes, He did. He once got so mad that people were treating His Father's temple like a marketplace that He started freaking out and flipping tables over. If Jesus can get that angry, it's okay for us too.

The key is that we can learn to feel our feelings without being controlled by them. We can acknowledge we are angry, feel that feeling, and even express it—but we can't use it as an excuse to sin. Anger is okay, but allowing our rage to hurt others with words or actions is *not okay*. But how do we keep ourselves in check, especially when we are super frustrated? It's not always easy. Sometimes when a situation or conversation is too intense and we can feel our temperature and temper rising, we need to create some space to cool off. When we cool off, we do two good things. First, we remove ourselves from the temptation to lash out, and second, we give ourselves enough space to think. When we involve our brain, we can problem solve instead of just reacting to our feelings. This prevents us from slipping into sin.

Whenever possible, try to make peace before bedtime. Even if it's a quick hug or a short phone call with a promise to resolve things more completely tomorrow, it's way better than nothing. God knows that going to bed angry can lead to a bitter, sleepless night. Tossing and turning in bed can invite all kinds of bad thoughts into our heads. This is what this verse means by "giving the enemy a foothold."

There is nothing wrong with anger. And there is nothing wrong with you if you feel angry. If you struggle with anger or frustration this week, pray to God and ask Him for help with self-control and problem solving. He will always help you work your way back to peace.

Mother

Through love and faithfulness sin is atoned for...
Proverbs 16:6

To understand this verse more deeply, we have to look at the essential difference between forgiveness and atonement. They are not the same thing, even though I read them as such when I first skimmed this chapter of Proverbs.

To attain forgiveness for sin, we must first be convicted of our sin (recognizing our brokenness and our mistakes, accepting our fault and responsibility), and conviction is a gift from the Holy Spirit. The Holy Spirit is the gut check and the finger point. It is that gnawing feeling that we cannot bury or rationalize away. After conviction comes repentance, the humble process of asking God for forgiveness. When we ask God with a humble heart and a contrite spirit, we are immediately forgiven. It's done. But there may still be work left to do on our part, and this process is called atonement.

Atonement is the process of making reparation for a wrong or injury; it consists of making amends. Sometimes atonement involves our words or actions toward a person we hurt, intentionally or unintentionally. When we cause pain unintentionally, it is no less painful to someone else;

it just means that perhaps in this case our intentions may have been better. We still must seek forgiveness and pursue atonement. Love is the basis behind atonement, and faithfulness is the application of that love over time. Like earning trust back, or apologizing for words that caused a fissure in relationship, or repairing or replacing something we've mishandled, broken, or lost—these things all take time. We must seek forgiveness from God, from the person, and finally we must learn to forgive ourselves and go on. The work of atonement is healthy and healing for everyone involved, just like forgiving someone who has hurt us is freeing for everyone involved.

We need to be more open about our own sin. We need to share our shortcomings with our daughters in order for them to better understand the full process of forgiveness, atonement, and freedom. If we are too ashamed of our own mistakes to openly walk our path of healing, our girls will miss vital lessons in their own spiritual growth.

Take the opportunity this week to share a situation with your daughter, a current challenge or a pitfall from your past. Explain to her how bad you felt before you had the sense and courage to take your sinfulness to God. Be explicit, not necessarily with the details of your sin, but with the steps you took to repair and restore the relationship or situation. Only by being open and willing to disclose our own sin will we ever have the basis for an honest relationship with our daughters in regard to theirs.

Daughter

Through love and faithfulness sin is atoned for...
Proverbs 16:6

Sin feels like a heavy weight. We can lug it around, try to hide it, or try to pretend it never happened, but we can no more escape our sin than we can escape our reflection when we look in the mirror. It's always there, looking back at us.

The bad feelings we have after we sin (stomachache, sleeplessness, stress, anxiety) are called conviction. This is when the Holy Spirit is telling us that we need to pay attention to something we did or said that caused God some grief. Chances are, we already know it wasn't right. We may have had that feeling moments afterward. The closer our relationship grows with God, the more quickly these feelings come. The only path to feeling free and good again is to go to God, confess our sins, and ask Him for forgiveness.

God grants forgiveness immediately when we go to Him with a humble and honest heart. Ask and you shall receive. *No matter what you did.* End of story. You are forgiven.

So the process goes—conviction (realizing we were wrong) and repentance (asking God for forgiveness), followed by atonement. Atonement is what we do to set things right again, our best attempt to fix things. If we borrow something from a friend and lose it or ruin it, we ask for forgiveness, but our atonement may be to use our own money and buy her a replacement. If we lie to our parents, our atonement may be a willing loss of privileges and slowly earning back their trust, one day at a time. If we betray the confidence of a friend, our atonement may be to calmly accept their anger and disappointment and work to restore trust and respect over time.

If someone isn't willing or ready to forgive us when we ask for it, we have to proceed anyway. We accept the almighty forgiveness of God and have faith that we are forgiven in His eyes. We use that power to help us to forgive ourselves. Then we go about the details, under God's direction, of cleaning up our mess.

If you have been ignoring the tug of the Holy Spirit, this is your week to accept that conviction and take a look at the sin you may have been avoiding. If you need guidance, ask your mom or your priest or pastor to show you how to navigate the path to peace.

Mother

> ... "If you hold to my teaching, you are really my
> disciples. Then you will know the truth, and the
> truth will set you free."
>
> *John 8:31–32*

When I was growing up, my father hammered three things
into his children: "Integrity. Responsibility. Judgment." No
matter what mistakes you made in our household, if you
told the truth about it, your consequences were far less
severe. Nothing you could do would ever be as bad as the
choice to tell a lie and cover it up. Dad always said that the
truth always comes out anyway, so it may as well come out
of you.

These were the words spoken at our house, but they were
also the way my parents lived. I cannot remember ever wit-
nessing a lapse of integrity in my parents. They weren't
perfect, of course, but integrity was never their stumbling
block. In our teenage years they even went so far as to say,
"If you are in a situation (at a party, with some friends, on a
date, anywhere) and you realize you are in over your head
or things have taken a turn you aren't comfortable with,
call us and we will get you—consequence-free, no matter
what."

I took them up on that on several occasions, and so did my friends. And because I knew that truth was always met with grace, no matter how ugly it was, I always chose it *because it set me free*. They lived the teaching of this verse.

In my adult years, I fumbled with my integrity and dropped the ball. I tested God on this verse, and the flames of my lessons left scars that I treasure today. I never want to forget what I learned. Both the way I was raised and my own sins affect my parenting today. I want my children to know this verse intimately. I want to model Christ's teachings for them by mandating truth, accepting truth even (especially) when it hurts, and enforcing consequences that allow grace for those with the courage to be honest.

We learn these lessons the hard way. We teach these lessons the intentional way.

Lord, in order for me to teach my daughters about integrity, my own must be refined. If there are any cracks in my integrity, help me to address them and fill them with Your Truth. Shine Your light into my heart and my past and help me make things right. May my own lessons be fuel for renewal—in my own life and in the raising of my children. Thank You for Your Word and for the freedom You purchased for me with Your own suffering. Be rigorous with me in my pursuit of truth, so that by living it and passing it on to my children, we will all be set free. In Your holy name, amen.

Are there areas of your own integrity that need repentance and refinement? Are you mindful about teachable moments, showing your daughter that her choices have consequences but her honesty makes them more tolerable? Show her in small ways to prepare her for the big.

Daughter

> ... "If you hold to my teaching, you are really my disciples. Then you will know the truth, and the truth will set you free."
>
> *John 8:31–32*

One day when I was in sixth grade, taking a test in my health class, my teacher had to leave the room for a minute. Everyone started talking the minute she left. She came back into the room, furious with us for breaking the rule to not talk during a test! She immediately said, "All right, who was talking? Raise your hands right now!"

I raised my hand, since I had said something to my friend.

I was the only one raising my hand—in a classroom full of talkers. Boy did I feel like a fool when I was the only kid who got detention.

At dinner that night, I had to tell my parents about my detention. Since I was typically such a quiet nerd, my whole family was very curious about how I got in trouble. I explained what happened, and I could see my Dad's face turning red. He was furious. I braced myself for his anger, thinking for sure I was about to get grounded. But I was mistaken. He was upset with me (a little, for talking), but he was really upset that my teacher punished me for my honesty and let everyone else off the hook with their lie.

My dad really has a thing about the truth. No matter what bad choices you can make, in his mind the worst one is lying.

The next morning, on his way to work, he stopped by the classroom to talk to my health teacher. He explained to her that in our family he and my mom worked very hard to make sure their children valued honesty, and he did not like the way she punished me for telling the truth. She was nervous and offered to take back my detention. "No," he said. "She was talking, that was wrong, and she will serve her detention. But think carefully next time about the lessons you teach and the values you want to reward." I have thought about that day many times over the years, and I bet my teacher has too.

God tells us that no matter how hard it is, the truth will always set us free in the end. When you have a choice to make, a decision about whether to tell the truth or lie, think of this verse. The truth might sting for a little while, but you are free afterward. A lie will haunt you and hurt you forever. Telling the truth leaves your mistakes in the past, where they belong. A lie carries them with you, and they get heavier and heavier to lug around.

This week, find ways to practice this verse in small things. Tell the truth about something, and watch how God rewards you with His peace. Make choices that define you as a person of integrity.

Mother

> Jesus turned and saw her. "Take heart, daughter," he said, "your faith has healed you." And the woman was healed at that moment.
>
> *Matthew 9:22*

There are many stories in the Bible related to healing. The common components involve a seeker, Jesus, an act of faith, and belief. The seeker may be seeking healing on his or her own behalf, on behalf of someone else, or even (like the woman at the well) almost resigned to his or her state of brokenness and feeling unworthy of any cure or redemption. In each case, the seeker encounters the presence of Jesus. An opportunity presents itself and he or she takes it, with an act of faith. Like the woman in this chapter of Matthew, who seeks a cure from her bleeding disorder and takes the opportunity to touch Jesus' cloak, or the friends who take the opportunity to lower their paralytic friend on a stretcher through the roof of a house in order to come in contact with Jesus, or the desperate man who cries out that his daughter has died, or the blind men who follow Jesus and cry out to Him to restore their sight.

We can see from examples in Scripture that when we

need healing we seek Jesus, we follow Him, we take the opportunity to present our need to Him, and finally we believe He is able to heal us.

Jesus even asks the blind men, "Do you believe I am able to do this?" They respond, "Yes, Lord." And Jesus replies, *"According to your faith* will it be done to you."

In the verse "Take heart, daughter, *your faith has healed you,"* it is a cooperative effort between the mighty power of Jesus and our faith that brings the real healing, the complete restoration. It isn't enough to simply ask for healing; we must *believe the Healer.*

Of course healing doesn't always come in the way we expect or desire, but we have to believe that it comes.

Are there areas of your heart, your family, or your life that have been in need of healing for some time now? Think about these areas this week. Follow the examples in Scripture from those who sought and received healing. Have you done enough? Have you sought Jesus, truly, with all your heart? Have you boldly made the effort to follow Him? Have you humbled yourself and asked for healing, presenting your pain and brokenness to Him?

And finally, perhaps the most important question of all, do you really believe that He is able to heal you? Maybe Jesus is waiting on you.

Do you really want to be healed? Do you really want healing for someone else? Go to God with an open and expectant heart. Have faith.

Daughter

> Jesus turned and saw her. "Take heart, daughter," he said, "your faith has healed you." And the woman was healed at that moment.
>
> *Matthew 9:22*

We see a lot of bad things in this broken world. We see families break up through divorce, people die from illness, people injured from accidents, animals and children who are abused and mistreated. For those without eyes of faith, it must seem like God doesn't care.

But for all the bad news out there, there is still plenty of good news. Miracles happen today just as they did more than two thousand years ago when Jesus walked on this planet. Sometimes we or someone we love could use a miracle. Broken hearts need to be mended. Cancers need to be cured. Bones need to heal. Babies need to live. Fevers need to break. Bullies need to be stopped. Disappointment needs to turn into joy.

There are so many examples of how we need healing. And there are so many good examples in the Bible of real people (like us) with real problems (like ours) who found Jesus and were healed. Injured people stopped bleeding, dead people opened their eyes, blind people saw, and paralyzed people stood up and walked. We can learn a lot about healing by paying attention to exactly what these people did. If you read chapter 9 of Matthew, you will see several examples.

These desperate folks who needed healing did several things. First, they found and followed Jesus. Once they found Him, they were not shy—they asked Him for help! Finally and most importantly, they believed that Jesus had the power to heal them. We can learn from these examples that no matter how often or how desperately we beg Jesus to help us, if we don't truly believe in our hearts that He can do it, it may not happen. Even if healing doesn't come the way we imagine or desire, it always comes in some way. *Our request must be made in faith and trust.*

Are you struggling with healing right now? Is there something you want Jesus to fix for you or for someone else? If you feel like nothing is happening, take some time this week to think about trusting Him with the outcome. We must believe in the healing, but, even more important, we must believe in the Healer.

Do you believe, without a doubt, that Jesus can do what He says He can do?

If so, tell Him.

Mother

> Bear with each other and forgive one another if any of you has a grievance against someone. Forgive as the Lord forgave you.
>
> *Colossians 3:13*

Nothing throws up a spiritual roadblock quite like unforgiveness. When we won't forgive, we are refusing and withholding all at once. We are refusing God's grace and mercy, basically shunning the gift Jesus gave us when He died for our sins. And we are withholding that grace from someone else. This creates a bottleneck of epic proportions, and we find ourselves going absolutely nowhere.

When we are stuck in that place of rationalizing our unforgiveness, we can come up with all kinds of good reasons why we simply cannot forgive someone or let their transgression go. We mull over our hurts and betrayals; we replay the insults and injuries of the past. We linger over our pain and reassure ourselves that the other person does not deserve our forgiveness.

The catch is that we do not deserve God's forgiveness either. He gave it as a gift. In fact, He gave His Son and His Son gave His life to bridge the gap between sin and freedom. When we look back over our own shortcomings and poor decisions, the way we ourselves have hurt people, there is no other reaction than humility followed by gratitude (and maybe a dash of wonder, for good measure). *Who am I, Lord, that You would forgive me and restore me to Your good grace?*

Who are we, indeed? We are just as sinful and undeserving as the next guy, maybe not in the exact same way, but just as broken. Once we have experienced the divine mercy of God, we have a better understanding of what is expected of us when it's our turn to forgive. We go and do likewise.

And if we struggle (we will), we can simply view it as a matter of obedience. God says to forgive, and so I must. The beauty is that immediately upon releasing someone else, we find that we too are free. Obedience always yields a clattering of opened shackles.

Are there areas where you are stuck, mired in unforgiveness? Are there places in your heart that you have let fester, bitterness that has gone unchecked and unresolved? Involve your daughter in the process of the work you are undertaking. Let her know what you have held on to and why it's finally time to let go. Show her what obedience looks like, step by step. When she comes to you with a confession, be quick to forgive her too. Most of all, let her know and let her see that you accept God's forgiveness and are able to turn around and forgive yourself. Girls who don't understand this grow into women who don't live it. Chains beget chains. Do you want a liberated legacy? Then start breaking free.

Daughter

> Bear with each other and forgive one another if any of you has a grievance against someone. Forgive as the Lord forgave you.
>
> *Colossians 3:13*

When someone hurts us, it's easy to hold a grudge. Every time we think about that person, we are reminded of whatever they did that made us so hurt or mad. Maybe they let us down; maybe they said or did something really mean; maybe they broke our trust or betrayed our friendship. Whatever they did, it wasn't nice.

If we aren't careful, we can let hurt grow roots, and this is what turns into bitterness. The thing about bitterness is that once you allow it to grow in the garden of your heart, it grows fast, taking up all the light and nutrients, causing beautiful things to wither and die. When we forgive someone who hurt us, that root of bitterness is pulled right out of our heart like a weed. Now we have sun and soil for good things to grow.

God knows what we need to do for our own good. That is why He tells us in His word that we are to forgive the way He has forgiven us. When we ask God for forgiveness,

He forgives us immediately. He instructs us to do the same thing for others. Because God knows that if we don't forgive, we are punishing ourselves as much as the people we want to punish. Isn't this silly? We think we are putting them in a jail of unforgiveness, but realize soon enough that we have actually locked ourselves in. When we refuse to forgive people, we are holding on to whatever they did to hurt us. The memory of that hurt replays over and over, and we continue to experience that pain again and again.

The only way to break free is to let those people go. Immediately, once we obey God and forgive, they no longer have power over us; they can no longer hurt us. We are free—because we set them free.

This week, think and talk about the subject of forgiveness. Are there people in your life you refuse to forgive? Are there painful words or moments that you replay over and over again? Imagine being free of these people and memories. If you decide to forgive but are having trouble figuring out how to let it go, pray to God and ask Him to help you. Allow your mom, your dad, or your priest or pastor to advise you on the process of forgiveness and freedom.

Jesus died so you could be free—don't waste His precious gift.

Mother

> "The LORD himself goes before you and will be
> with you; he will never leave you nor forsake you.
> Do not be afraid; do not be discouraged."
>
> *Deuteronomy 31:8*

There is no fear quite like the fear of being abandoned or alone—particularly in our time of need. Being abandoned by another person creates a wound that, without God, is impossible to heal. It creates a cavern in the heart that eradicates the ability to trust or truly open up.

Some of you reading today experienced this type of abandonment. I have friends who are still struggling today, as middle-aged adults, because they were abandoned by a parent when they were young. I have other friends who were abandoned by a dear friend, sibling, or husband, and their ache is deep and profound. I have friends who felt abandoned when their parent died, other friends who felt abandoned by the effects of divorce, and other friends who experienced abandonment via an empty nest when the kids went to college. I want you to know that I approach this subject today with extreme tenderness and humility. There are few places more vulnerable in the human heart than the raw areas created by loss.

Interestingly, the aftershocks of abandonment can go on to do greater and more sustained damage than the original loss. Left unhealed, abandonment goes on to punish other people and wreck other relationships. Sometimes it can cause us to be utterly unable to open our hearts to new and solid relationships, simply because the unhealed areas cannot bear the possible risk of future pain. We conclude in our broken thinking that if someone has left us before, we must not be worth sticking around for. So we shut down and shut off.

This is living an approximation of life and love. This is not what God intends for you. Deep wounds require deep healing and restoration, and this is possible only with God. We can have a new heart and a new mind in Christ; we can love in new and healthy ways; and we can think better thoughts. But we have to be willing to lay it all out before the Lord.

Everyone has some area of abandonment, big or small. This week I want you to go there and take a look at yours because only by going there, and then taking it all to God, do we have any hope for healing. Abandoned people tend to abandon others. Is this really a risk you are willing to take? The thought of letting down a loved one might be impetus enough to go deep.

The only way to heal the wound of abandonment is by trusting our healing to the One who will never leave us.

Daughter

> "The LORD himself goes before you and will be with you; he will never leave you nor forsake you. Do not be afraid; do not be discouraged."
>
> *Deuteronomy 31:8*

It's a sad but true thought, but every single person we love is going to let us down occasionally. Even sadder and truer, we are going to let down the people we love sometimes.

When someone lets us down—doesn't show up, forgets something important to us, isn't there when we need them, doesn't return our important phone call or email—we can feel unimportant or unloved. But in reality, no human being has enough love to give us everything we need. Our needs are too much, too deep, for another person to fill. God designed us this way so we wouldn't put any person in His place. Only God has enough time to listen to every single one of our problems or fears. Only God has enough patience to hear our stories and requests over and over. Only God has enough love to fill our hearts completely. Only God has enough strength to continue to carry us through the rough spots in life.

If we truly understand that God will never leave us or forget about us, it sets us free from putting these kinds of expectations on other people. That way, if they let us down or leave, we weren't completely relying on them in the first place. We know that only God can uphold a promise as big as that one. When we fill up on God's love, everyone else's love is a bonus, like a gift. We don't expect it, or even need it—it's just really nice. In fact, when we put less pressure on people, we set them free to be human, rather than setting them up to be perfect.

When we trust God to never leave us, we are free of the fear of being left or being alone. We don't have to worry about the future and what might happen because we know we will never have to face it alone—no matter what happens, we are going to be okay. When we worry less, we can be free to live our life in the present moment. We can enjoy the day today and we can enjoy the people we are with. God gives us life in twenty-four-hour days because we couldn't handle bigger chunks of time than that. We were never supposed to live in the past (our memories) or live in the future (our worries or our dreams of what might be). Our life is right here, right now. And God is with us. Always.

Lord, help me to trust You more. Help me to take the most tender places of my heart to You first. I know You will never leave me or forget me, and because of that I have confidence and peace that cannot be shaken—no matter what. Thank You for loving me this way. In Jesus' name I pray, amen.

Mother

> ... "If you do not stand firm in your faith, you will not stand at all."
>
> **Isaiah 7:9**

Nourishing our faith and tending to our spiritual growth can get pushed aside by the demands of life when things seem to be going smoothly. But a sudden shift in circumstance, the onset of a fiery trial, can bring the crumbling awareness that we have spent our time on the wrong things. We are not prepared. We haven't been fortified by Scripture or strengthened by prayer and time spent with God. Perhaps even the friendships we have fostered prove to be insufficient in our hour of need. All our weak spots are revealed when we experience a season of sifting.

I love how Oswald Chambers describes ordinary times as time to spend with God in the "workroom." He explains that if we do our work here, we will be strong and sufficient for ourselves when a trial comes—but more important, we will be useful to someone else who is struggling.

I believe that as mothers, we are required to spend quality time in the workroom. We cannot be weak and flimsy in our faith when a crisis hits. When the seas churn and the skies go black, we are supposed to be the lighthouse on the shore, a steady guide back to safety. It does no good at all for two inexperienced sailors to attempt to row around in the waves in a dark storm. Both boats would end up crushed on the rocks. The storm might be a crisis, a challenging season or set of circumstances, or it might be as simple as the waves of adolescence. Whatever it is, this Scripture speaks to moms: "If we don't stand firm in our faith, we won't stand at all."

Think about the kind of steadiness you want to offer your daughter. In her moment of need, what kind of mother will you be? Will you be strong enough to support her? To carry her, if needed? Do you have what it takes to withstand the storms of life and offer shelter for your family? Are you the bright, reliable, guiding light on the shore?

Think about the workroom this week. If you are blessed with ordinary times right now, use them in an extraordinary way. Figure out a plan to fortify your faith. Act as though a storm is coming and you need to secure supplies and batten down the hatches. Spend time with God in prayer. Seek guidance from God's Word. Pray with your daughter. Nourish your friendships with faithful friends.

Ask God to show you how to strengthen yourself so you will be able to stand firm.

People are counting on you.

Daughter

> ... "If you do not stand firm in your faith, you will not stand at all."
>
> *Isaiah 7:9*

There are ordinary times, and there are extraordinary times.

Ordinary times are just regular life; you get up, go to school or work, see friends, play sports, do what you normally do. Time seems to pass at a regular pace, and if all we've ever known are ordinary times, we might mistakenly label them as "boring." It's hard to be grateful for ordinary when you don't know the difference—yet.

Extraordinary times usually take us by surprise. Something unexpected happens, and life throws us a test. Storms, illness, accident, tragedy, temptation, a broken relationship, any challenge or difficulty—these all make for extraordinary times. Extraordinary times reveal our strength and our character. Extraordinary times prove our faith—is our faith solid and reliable, or were we simply going through the motions? If we were just going through the motions, our faith is flimsy and weak right when we need it the most. When temptation or peer pressure strike, that moment is too late to fortify your faith; it has to be there already. You may not have time to pause and pray; you have to already be walking closely with God and tuned into His voice.

Extraordinary times, if we are open to God, can also prove our faith. Testing times can be a wake-up call to make some changes. Maybe we can learn about the value of real friends or the value of time spent with God in prayer or at church. Hard times shake everything up, and when things are shaking, it's very clear what remains steady. Ultimately, you want to be one of the steady ones. The time to train for that is today.

If you are in a season of ordinary times right now, make use of it! Do what you can do now so that you will be able to stand firm when life shakes you up. Spend time with faithful friends. Spend time with God; pray and look for God's answers in the Bible. Go to church, even when you might rather sleep in. Think about how to best use ordinary time. When extraordinary times come, your faith will be revealed and you will be fit and strong.

You will be able to help yourself, as well as your friends and your family. You will be able to stand firm.

Mother

> At that time Jesus said, "I praise you, Father, Lord of heaven and earth, because you have hidden these things from the wise and learned, and revealed them to little children. Yes, Father, for this is what you were pleased to do."
>
> *Matthew 11:25–26*

As a grown-up, it's easy to assume what we think we know. We have walked with God for years. We have done Bible studies. We have sat in church on too many Sundays to count. We pray with our friends. We talk to God throughout the day. We count all our knowledge and all our experience as our wisdom and we rely on it as truth.

The small issue is that we do not possess truth. *Jesus* is the way, the truth, and the life. And while we do have some knowledge and some experience, wisdom is acquired bit by bit over a lifetime. We can become blinded and jaded by *what we think we know*. We can assume that what worked in the past is the solution for the future, regardless of the timing or situation. We can get stuck.

There have been many moments in my parenting when one of my children said something that absolutely leveled me. Maybe they pulled the rug of my pride right out from under me. Maybe they pointed out a blind spot in my thinking. Maybe they spoke truth to me that was so simple and pure that I overlooked it in favor of my complex reasoning and missed the point entirely. Children can call a spade a spade, a fraud a fraud, a liar a liar. They can point and remark that the emperor is naked because they are just stating the obvious. They speak openly regarding their intuition (which is the Holy Spirit, after all), and it isn't layered with the buildup of years, manners, or customs. We might be tempted to ignore our intuition, or glaze over it with social niceties, and open ourselves to risk. The Holy Spirit speaks. And often the Spirit speaks through the mouths of children.

We have to unclog our ears (the pride and the buildup of what we think we know) and be able to listen. Good leaders always listen to their people. They are always open to suggestion or new information. The moment we think we know everything is precisely when we will trip and fall over something we didn't see or expect.

A good parent has to know when to exercise authority and when to be open to adjustment. Power comes from God, not from control. Spend some time this week asking God to reveal your blind spots. Be open to hearing what you don't know that you don't know. Humility is the catalyst to growth, so be willing to humble yourself. Let your daughter know that you want to hear her perspective, and then really listen. You may be surprised that she has wisdom of her own to share; that her knowledge and experience are different, and valid. Share your collective wisdom, and practice going to God together for answers instead of pretending that you know.

Daughter

> At that time Jesus said, "I praise you, Father, Lord of heaven and earth, because you have hidden these things from the wise and learned, and revealed them to little children. Yes, Father, for this is what you were pleased to do."
>
> *Matthew 11:25–26*

Since God actually does know everything, imagine how annoying it must be to Him when puny little people think that they know it all. God has His own ways of giving wisdom to His people.

He gives wisdom to those who seek it. Nowhere does it say that God gives wisdom to people *of a certain age*.

Don't you love that about our God? No one is too old to be used by Him, and no one is too young. Even Paul says to his young friend Timothy, don't let anyone look down on you because you are young. Being young is not a limitation to God, nor is it an excuse.

Even though young people are expected to be respectful of authority, it doesn't mean that you cannot or should not respectfully speak up when you have an opinion or an idea. In fact, learning to express yourself in front of adults will serve to increase both your experience and your maturity.

Sometimes simply because you are young, you will have a new angle or a fresh perspective that would be incredibly helpful in finding a solution or a compromise.

When God gives you a good idea, speak your truth! Don't be ashamed or shy because of your age. A good idea is a good idea—period. It has nothing to do with the age of the person who came up with it. In fact, God may use your fine mind to further His perfect plans. If He sees fit to use you, be honored, humble, and ready. Never think that you can't, or that you have to wait until you are grown to earn the right to be heard.

God values you, right now, as much as anyone else. Take strength and confidence from that unconditional, timeless love.

This week, think of any situations where you felt scared or too shy to speak your mind or offer your idea. Plan to be bolder next time. Ask God to increase your wisdom and your confidence. The future depends on good leaders—and this means you! Learn everything you can.

Mother

> "Before I formed you in the womb I knew you, before you were born I set you apart; I appointed you as a prophet to the nations."
>
> *Jeremiah 1:5*

If you ever had any questions about your place or purpose in God's plan, allow your heart to steep in this verse like a strong cup of tea. If you sometimes feel like you are just going through the motions, with one day bleeding into the next without a discernable purpose other than your to-do list, take heart. God set Jeremiah apart, *and God set you apart*. He has a special appointment for you and for your daughter.

It's almost too awesome to consider that God knew you before you were formed. He had a specific agenda in mind with your design, creating you to fill a certain niche in this particular time in history. Nothing about you is haphazard or random. You are gifted in an exact way that is like no one else. No one else can do the things you do, the way you do them, and touch the people in your sphere of influence. It's up to you.

If you play small, shrink back, or hide, there is a noticeable gap in our Kingdom. We waste so much time comparing our gifts to others that we can neglect our individual growth and appointed contribution. God gives you gifts so that you can share them.

If you aren't sure what your gifts are, *ask*. Ask God. Ask trusted confidantes to pray and ask God on your behalf. Remember the things that have always brought you joy. The joy is key because when you are doing what you love, joy is the overflow. God created you to love doing the thing He created you to do. You cannot live a fully actualized life if you are neglecting your appointment. God did not create you for an approximation. He created you to be set apart.

This week, challenge yourself to spend time in prayer each morning. Ask God to show you how to cultivate your gifts and where to share your strength. Begin to pray in earnest for your daughter's gifts to be revealed to her. Ask God to help you help her. When your daughter sees you living a full-spectrum life, using your gifts to bring glory to God, it serves as an inspiration for her to do likewise.

What are the things you have always loved to do? When and where do you feel God's favor shine upon you?

What activities energize you rather than deplete you?

How are you tempted to shrink back or play small, minimizing your calling?

What do you believe God set you apart to do? How can you live your appointment in full view of your daughter?

Daughter

> "Before I formed you in the womb I knew you, before you were born I set you apart; I appointed you as a prophet to the nations."
>
> *Jeremiah 1:5*

Did you know that God thought long and hard about *you*, long before you were ever born?

He knew exactly what you would look like, the things you would like to do, where you would live, who your family and friends would be, and the exact date of your birthday. Nothing God does is by accident—our God is a God of purpose. And He has a specific purpose in mind for you.

God created you to love certain things, and chances are, over time, the things you love will become the things you are good at. Our purpose and our passion usually end up going in the same direction. The more things you try, the more you will be able to figure out the things you love. That is why you should never feel shy or embarrassed to try new things, whether you succeed or fail, whether you end up liking them or disliking them. It's all part of the process of figuring out the part you will play in God's Kingdom. No one can play your part but you.

In fact, if you don't try, or if you hide your talents, there is a missing spot with your name on it. God appointed you to be *you*, to do *your thing* at this specific time in history. He has certain people that can only be influenced by you. But you have to be out there, fulfilling your destiny, in order to be in the right place at the right moment.

Growing up is all about *growing into* the person God designed you to become. The more you pray to Him to reveal details about yourself and your purpose, the more quickly and easily you will move in the right direction. Bring all your questions, ideas, and details to God, and He will light the path He intended for you. Walk with Him into your future.

What are the things you really love to do? Do you see how God gifted you to do these certain things?

How do your gifts affect other people? How can you use them for good and God's glory?

How does knowing that God had you in mind long before you were born affect the way you see yourself?

Mother

And the LORD said to Joshua, "Today I will begin to exalt you in the eyes of all Israel, so they may know that I am with you as I was with Moses. Tell the priests who carry the ark of the covenant: 'When you reach the edge of the Jordan's waters, go and stand in the river.'"

Joshua 3:7–8

I once heard something that changed my view of my faith: *God doesn't call the equipped; He equips the called.* The bottom line is this: We have to step out in faith and obedience before we will ever feel ready. Obedience is the catalyst for God's power. We start walking, and He shows up.

Chapter 3 of Joshua is an excellent example of this faith phenomenon. The Israelites who were carrying the precious Ark of the Covenant had to trust Joshua's advice and literally step into the rushing floodwaters of the Jordan River before God stopped the flowing water and allowed them to walk across. If they had just stayed on the side and waited for a break in the current, they might still be standing there today. Instead, the entire nation of Israel was able to cross over a flooded river on dry ground.

Where is God calling you to cross over? Why are you refusing to take the first step of faith?

You may never feel ready. You may never have the level of confidence or skill you think you need in order to do the thing that God is calling you to do. You may never think that the timing is right. You may not ever believe that you are the one to do the task at hand. You may never think you have what it takes. Courage doesn't necessarily mean being fearless; it may mean being afraid but going for it anyway!

God isn't nearly as concerned with your feelings as He is with your obedience. It isn't about whether your strength or skill will be enough because it isn't your strength or skill that you will need—it's His. Step forward toward the thing He is asking you to do, and see how He shows up. He will equip you sufficiently for each step of faith.

What obstacle is currently in your path?

Pinpoint where you are allowing fear to hold you back.

If God is calling you to cross over, He has something amazing in mind for you on the other side. Are you willing to trust Him?

Pray for a spirit of obedience and ask God how and when to take your first step.

Daughter

> And the LORD said to Joshua, "Today I will begin to exalt you in the eyes of all Israel, so they may know that I am with you as I was with Moses. Tell the priests who carry the ark of the covenant: 'When you reach the edge of the Jordan's waters, go and stand in the river.'"
>
> *Joshua 3:7–8*

The traveling Israelites had a big obstacle to face: How to get across the Jordan River during flood season? They were also carrying precious cargo: the sacred Ark of the Covenant, which carried the original Ten Commandments.

There is something very important to notice about this Scripture. When the Israelites got closer to the edge of the river, God did not automatically part the water so that they could keep right on walking. God could have done that, but He did not. Instead He told Joshua to tell the people to walk into the flooded river. Can you imagine a rushing, flooded current? Can you imagine worrying about what might happen to the Ark, which was a huge responsibility? I bet the Israelites were frightened they might float away and lose the Ark forever.

But here's the thing—*God wanted His people to trust Him.*

And that's the same thing God wants for us to do today. When we have a big challenge to face, God wants us to go to Him for help. And many times He will have us take a step of faith, even before we think we are ready, or even when we don't know what will happen next. When we step out in the direction of God's leading, He meets us there. He responds to our obedience and our trust in Him with His powerful help—just when we need it the most.

As soon as the Israelites started walking into the river, God began to separate the water and create a dry path for them to cross. What do you think would have happened if they had just stood there, scared, and did not believe God enough to get their feet wet? They may never have completed their journey at all!

God wants us to obey Him. He wants us to trust Him enough to take the first step, knowing He will be there for us.

What is blocking your path these days? Do you have a certain challenge ahead? Is there a certain person or situation that is bothering you? Talk to God about it. Ask your mom to pray with you about it. If God reveals a solution to you, obey Him, and see what happens!

Does the idea of obeying God in tough situations scare you a little bit? Do you think you trust Him as much as you could?

Mother

> **I can do all this through him who gives me strength.**
>
> *Philippians 4:13*

The only words as powerful as "I can" are "I can't." The words we use to speak to ourselves become our truth. If you don't believe you can do something, chances are you truly cannot. I think the words "I can't" are often more a matter of "I won't." And if that is a more accurate statement, we need to own it.

There are plenty of things *I* cannot do, but when I cooperate with God, *we* can accomplish amazing things. God's power is made perfect in our weakness, so when we go to Him at the end of our rope, He ties a loop around our waists and never lets go.

I memorized this verse and I keep it handy when I am in the middle of a moment that seems too big for me. I have repeated this verse over and over in a rapid, panicked mantra at the end of a marathon. When I have nothing left to give, my calves are seizing up in cramps, and the finish line seems years away, I know that I can't make it, alone. It is in this moment that this verse speaks power into my weakness. And with God's help, I can endure. I say it when my kids are fighting and I'm about to lose it. I say it when I'm freaking out on a turbulent airplane. I say it when someone who annoys me corners me in conversation. I say it when I am about to step up to the podium and give a speech or interview. There's no way I can get up and talk in front of strangers, but we (God and I) can.

This verse simply must be part of your spiritual arsenal. And it is worthy of passing along to your daughter. As a mother, you cannot always be there when your daughter has a crisis or sudden moment of anxiety. Maybe she cringes when called on in class. Maybe she is about to run a race, or try out for the school play. Maybe she gets major jitters before a test. You can't stand on the starting line beside her. You can't sit in the desk next to her in school. But God can, and He does. We have to teach our girls how to connect to Him in their moments of weakness. Teach this verse to your daughter this week. Memorize it together. Say it out loud. Share the opportunities you have to use it. Remind her when she leaves for the day that she can do all things through Christ, who strengthens her.

Do you generally have an "I can" or "I can't" mentality?

Do you view your weaknesses with disdain and frustration, or do you see them as an opportunity to tap into God's power?

Have you already memorized this verse? If not, write it down and put it in several places this week where you and your daughter will see it. Practice saying it and relying upon it—out loud.

Daughter

> I can do all this through him who gives me strength.
>
> *Philippians 4:13*

My daughters are in a Bible study that meets once a month. One particular month they met just before two days of standardized testing at their school—one day for reading, the other day for math. It was the first time they had taken tests like these, and everyone was pretty nervous about it, not knowing what to expect or how well they might do. Every girl wanted to do her best.

Their Bible study teacher gave them this verse as a gift, and she told them to write it down and memorize it. She said it was as important as everything else they had learned all year, and perhaps learning to use this verse is an even bigger test than the one they were about to take! Here's the reason: If you believe you can do something, you probably can. If you think you can't, you are always right. It's over before you ever start. Believing that you can't means that you give up at the starting line. Believing that you can do anything *with God's help* is hugely powerful. It is also humble because you are admitting that you need God in order to succeed.

The girls in the Bible study memorized this verse. We had it written on sticky notes all around our house. My daughters said it out loud to each other, to me, and to themselves. On the day the testing started, they wrote 4:13 in Sharpie marker on their arms. It is an awesome verse to memorize and keep handy for whenever you feel nervous, when you get called on in class, when you try out for a play, when you are about to run a race, or when your team is about to start a game. Jitters are normal. A bit of nerves is a good thing because it means you care about what you are about to do. But when you let your nervousness remind you of your need for God, your weakness is transformed into power. God wants you to recognize how much you need His help. He wants to help you, and He wants to celebrate every victory with you and comfort you in any defeat. You can do all things, win or lose, with Christ at your side, keeping you strong.

Make a point this week to memorize this verse. Your mom is memorizing it too. Write it down and post it around the house where you both can see it. Write 4:13 on your hand or in your notebook. Practice saying it before you leave for school, or say it in your head any time you feel uncomfortable or afraid. Watch how God shows up for you when you need Him. Notice how your confidence grows when you speak strong words of faith to yourself.

You can do all things through Christ who strengthens you. Change your fear into power through 4:13.

Believe that God will help you.

Mother

> ...I have learned to be content whatever the circumstances. I know what it is to be in need, and I know what it is to have plenty. I have learned the secret of being content in any and every situation, whether well fed or hungry, whether living in plenty or in want.
>
> *Philippians 4:11–12*

Paul definitely learned the secret to contentment, and he puts it out there for us to share. So why are so many people living with a lack of contentment?

Our commercialized society propagates the "I'll be happy when..." mentality. We think that if we could just achieve this, lose this, buy this, or have this, then everything would be perfect. Once we achieve or get one thing, another thing looms or lures us on the horizon, and we are never at peace. We never stop to enjoy the thing we longed for previously. We are always on to the next thing. We mistakenly believe that happiness is about more and next, when perhaps it's about *less and now.*

We use words like "happiness" a lot, but the use of "contentment" is rare. I believe that many people associate contentment with something lazy or dull, like complacency. Like if you are content, you have somehow quit or given up. Given up striving, perhaps, but that is a good thing!

Contentment is more akin to peace than complacency. And if we don't actively take steps to rewire our brain and reprogram our heart to that end, we will constantly be pouring more and more (effort and materialism) into a bottomless pitcher and wondering why we are parched.

A lack of gratitude could be the original germ that caused the contentment illness of our culture. When we are living in such a way that we realize that *every single thing* we have is a gift from God, we are less proprietary and prideful. Our lack of entitlement allows us to be better equipped to handle challenges and to view our blessings as beautiful, bountiful overflow. We are thankful regardless. We can usually shift our stance and perspective enough to find a bright side in everything. We start to expect, and eventually need, less, and as a result we begin to have more—more of the things that really matter, the things that cannot be taken or fade away. Our lack of expectation regarding things and outcomes translates into a lack of expectation toward other people. This ultimately yields peace and acceptance, which looks a lot like love and contentment. Stop. Trying. So. Hard. Begin to appreciate where you are, what you are, how you are, and who you are—today.

How can you create an atmosphere of contentment in your heart and in your home? Are you living a model of gratitude for your family?

How do you handle setbacks? Blessings? How can you begin to live in such a way that you handle them more similarly and gracefully?

Daughter

> ...I have learned to be content whatever the circumstances. I know what it is to be in need, and I know what it is to have plenty. I have learned the secret of being content in any and every situation, whether well fed or hungry, whether living in plenty or in want.
>
> *Philippians 4:11–12*

Our culture today gives us a constant message of *more*.

Advertisements on television, in magazines, and on the Internet tell us that we need this product or that product in order to be satisfied. The thing is, once we get the thing we wanted, we go on to want something else. The idea of being satisfied by things is a total lie, but that is how companies get us to keep buying more stuff. Instead of being happier with our pile of stuff, we get lonelier and more buried beneath it. In our hurry to get more and more things, we forget the simple things that make us happy and cost nothing at all.

That is why Paul talks about contentment, rather than happiness, in this Scripture passage. Contentment is something more special, more rare, than just happiness. Happiness can depend more on good luck or good circumstances, whereas contentment means that you are at peace no matter what's going on or what you have.

If we don't recognize that our deepest need is not for things, or even for things to go smoothly, but for God alone, we will never be satisfied. It would be like eating and eating but never feeling full—eventually you would just feel sick. And we become sick in a way, when we are never content.

So how do we learn to be content? I believe that contentment comes from gratitude, from being thankful for everything, no matter what. We can always find a way to thank God, for the good things He gives us as well as for the challenges and difficulties. We can thank Him that hard times make us stronger and deepen our faith. If we can't think of anything else, we can even simply thank Him that things aren't any worse. There is always a way to find something to be grateful for. The more you begin to practice being thankful, the less you will want and the more content you will be. You will begin to see the gifts *you already have* with fresh eyes.

Another way to grow in contentment is to think about other people. When we focus on others instead of ourselves and find ways to show kindness to those in need, we automatically think less about our own needs. We become more aware of all the ways that God has already taken care of us, and we remember to say thank you.

Do you feel like there is always something you want? Do you ever feel jealous about the things that other people have? Would you like to be more content right now? This week make a list of all the things you are thankful for, big and small. Start thinking about ways you can serve others instead of serving yourself.

Mother

> Those who live according to the flesh have their
> minds set on what the flesh desires; but those
> who live in accordance with the Spirit have their
> minds set on what the Spirit desires. The mind
> governed by the flesh is death, but the mind gov-
> erned by the Spirit is life and peace.
>
> *Romans 8:5–6*

Funny how our circumstances can be virtually the same
but our moods can be so different from one day to the next.
One day we can feel capable and grateful, and the next we
are hopeless and overwhelmed. What is the deal?

The days that we are at peace are the days where our
thoughts have been aligned with the Holy Spirit. The days
we don't are the days we have succumbed to the temptation
to let the enemy run amok in our minds. Think about it—
the thoughts we have affect our feelings, and our emotions
affect our actions. If we want to get a handle on ourselves,
we have to go to the source: our thought life.

Negative self-talk is not just a bad mood; it is a bigger problem than that. The words we speak to ourselves can become
the truth we believe. *I'm not good enough, smart enough, thin
enough, capable enough, lovable enough. I can't. I'm stuck in*

this place. It's hopeless. I'm not enough. These are dangerous thoughts. Do you remember being a little girl and your mom or grandma telling you, "Don't make that ugly face; it might stick like that"? Well, I'm telling us not to think or say those ugly words, or *we* may stick like that. We have to let the Spirit control our thought life. At the first sign of negativity or enemy infiltration in our minds, we have to stop everything and address it. *Holy Spirit, come into my thought life now. Speak truth and silence the voice of oppression and lies.* If we can't stop the thought, there is no way we can halt the onslaught of emotion and the actions that ensue. By then it's simply too late. It takes a lot longer to stop a train going at full speed.

Once, with God's mighty help, we gain mastery over our thoughts, we will be better able to teach our daughters to do the same.

Do you suffer from runaway thoughts and negative thought patterns? Do they come out as words your daughter can hear or actions she can see? Are you ready to make a change?

If so, this week make a point to stop yourself every time you start going down the dark path of thinking. Ask the Holy Spirit to change your mind. Replace negative thoughts with hopeful ones, even if it's as simple as, God, I have made bad decisions before but today is a new day, and with Your help, I can do it differently starting right now. I am hopeful because You are beside me. Anything can change if my thoughts change. Help me. In Jesus' name, amen.

Daughter

> Those who live according to the flesh have their minds set on what the flesh desires; but those who live in accordance with the Spirit have their minds set on what the Spirit desires. The mind governed by the flesh is death, but the mind governed by the Spirit is life and peace.
>
> *Romans 8:5–6*

A mindset is a very important thing. If we have a positive mindset, we can try anything with a chance for success. However, with a negative mindset we can fail long before we ever really start. If we think we cannot do something, chances are we cannot.

What is the voice like in your head? How do you speak to yourself? Do you tell yourself hopeful, encouraging things, or do you talk to yourself in a mean or critical way? If you make a mistake, are you more apt to think, *Hey, it's okay. I tried. Next time I will know more and do it better.* Or are your thoughts more like this: *How could I make such an embarrassing mistake? I am such a failure. No way am I trying that again.* It's really important to understand the power of the way we speak to ourselves. Listen to the voice of your thoughts this week and be honest about the way you talk to yourself.

The Holy Spirit can help us control our thoughts. This is important because what we think affects the way we feel, and the way we feel affects our actions. So if our thoughts are messed up, our actions likely will be too. It's hard to overcome our feelings when our thoughts have already taken them off track in a negative way. If we can catch ourselves earlier, at the first few thoughts in a negative direction, we can ask the Spirit to help us change our thoughts and our path. New thoughts mean new actions and new results.

No one responds well to negativity. An overweight person who is teased may eat more. A person who struggles in math won't get better grades if the teacher calls him or her stupid. The same goes for you. What you say to yourself matters. It changes how you see yourself, the way others see you, and what you are able to accomplish. Be careful about the words you choose this week and see what changes for you.

How would you describe the voice in your head? How do you talk to yourself?

Could you be more positive and encouraging to yourself? Ask the Holy Spirit to help you change the way you think, so it is more in line with the way God thinks. Your mind can be renewed, with God's help!

Mother

> **The churning inside me never stops; days of suf-
> fering confront me.**
>
> *Job 30:27*

When I go through periods of acute stress, this is exactly how I feel. My stomach churns nonstop, I can't sleep, and I alternate between lack of appetite and eating anything in front of me. And let's be clear: Any suffering I have encountered has been nothing compared to what Job endured.

If I were to be perfectly honest, I would say that part of my stress related to suffering probably comes from my resistance to it. I go through the pitiful phases *Why me?* and *Why this?* Somehow in the face of my own suffering I forget that the earth is not heaven. I forget that no one said that living a Christian life would be easy all the time; in fact, I was promised the opposite. Perhaps it is the very essence of my whiny entitlement that God is trying to eradicate when He allows for seasons of difficulty in my life. What if we viewed suffering as a compliment instead of punishment? What if we could wrap our heads around the notion that God wants to refine us for something special?

I love the saying that God is more interested in our character than our comfort. Thank goodness for that fact because left to my own devices I am quite certain I would be more interested in my comfort. And how boring is that, really? But humans are weak by nature, and we do seek comfort over our own development when we aren't aligned with God. We forget that it is suffering that makes us more Christ-like, suffering that burns the chaff and refines us like silver. Without suffering there is no real growth. Pleasure perhaps brings gratitude (ideally), but not real growth.

Maturity is attained by an openness to growth, and this includes meeting suffering with some measure of welcome. We may not like it, but we may as well face it. It comes either way, whether we meet it or run and hide. Denial may be cheaper than therapy, as the cocktail napkins say, but it is at the expense of spiritual growth.

And that, my dear, we simply cannot afford.

How do you initially react to a challenge or difficulty? Do you experience a period of denial, resistance, or resentment? How do you handle this?

How would you like to handle seasons of suffering in the future? The only way to change our patterns is by reworking them in smaller situations with less on the line. This week, practice new patterns of dealing with minor disappointments. Shift your perspective to seek growth over comfort.

If God wants to work on your character, try being flattered rather than frustrated.

Daughter

> The churning inside me never stops; days of suf-
> fering confront me.
>
> *Job 30:27*

This verse perfectly describes that nervous feeling we all get in the pit of our stomach when we are anxious or uncomfortable. Churning is a great word for it; our insides are turning flips, and our minds are whirling with stressful thoughts.

I remember being the new kid at school when I was young. We moved thirteen times, so this was a common feeling for me. I was shy and awkward, so every time I had to start over again, figure out a new school, and meet new friends, it was a pretty big deal. It wasn't really suffering, in the true sense, but it caused me plenty of stress!

I think about the alternative: What would have happened if I never moved at all? I think I would still be shy and quiet, never having had a need to get over it. My family probably wouldn't be as close as we are. I wouldn't have the spirit of adventure that I have today. I might not be as open to meeting new people. I probably wouldn't love to travel. I might not love foreign languages the way I do. There are all kinds of things that would likely be very different about my life. I can see now, looking back, that God was preparing me for the life I live today.

Whenever God allows for suffering, or even seasons of feeling uncomfortable, He has a bigger purpose in mind. He is more interested in our character than in our comfort. There are certain ways you need to grow and change, and those things can happen only by making you uncomfortable. If we aren't uncomfortable, we don't seek change and growth. We simply stay the same. God wants us to be open to the changes He has in store for us; He wants us to allow (and even invite) Him to develop and prepare us along the way.

Try to view challenging times as training times—God is training you to be ready for the rest of your life. If everything in your life were easy, you would be weak and unable to withstand future difficulties. Being a Christian is challenging, but it's also very exciting when we are open to God's possibilities. The more you grow, the more you won't want it any other way.

We will never be able to face big challenges if we don't prepare ourselves in the small ones. This week, when something doesn't go your way or feels uncomfortable, instead of resisting it, ask God to help you learn from it. Suffering gets a bad rap, but it's meant for our good.

Be open to what God has to teach you. Be encouraged because He is preparing you for important things.

Mother

> **It is for freedom that Christ has set us free. Stand firm, then, and do not let yourselves be burdened again by a yoke of slavery.**
>
> *Galatians 5:1*

Whenever I make a mistake, I first kick myself a thousand times, then I berate myself, then I dwell on it, rehash it, and play the what-if game. Then I tell my friends about it so I can make myself feel even worse. Then I come to my senses long enough to remember to ask God for forgiveness, and although I believe He has forgiven me, it takes me a lot longer to forgive myself.

Maybe on some level I believe that my bad decision requires a certain amount of penance time to "earn" back my good standing with God. Nothing could be further from the truth. No matter how hard I try, I could never, ever do anything sufficient enough to "earn" the grace He gives for free. It's a ridiculous notion, and I know it. His mercy is available at all times; the catch is getting myself to accept it and move on.

If Christ sets us free (from sin, from addiction, from our past, from a bad relationship, from old patterns, from old definitions of ourselves, from anything!) and we are still living in chains, that is our own sad problem. Christ did not set us free so that we would be living some approximation of a joyful life, slumped with bad posture caused by guilt and burdens. No way. He wants us to stand up tall and live joyfully and gratefully. That is precisely how we live a life that glorifies Him. We humbly and graciously accept the great gift He offers us, and we live our forgiveness and freedom large and out loud. And, listen closely, *we offer that same grace to others*. We are gloriously free, and we make it a point to set as many other people free as we go along.

I never really understood this until I had my children and they got old enough to express shame and flog themselves for a mistake. It truly broke my heart. It was then that I finally understood how God feels every time I refuse the gift of forgiveness and go on hating myself. I am determined to live a life of freedom and model forgiving others *and myself* so that my children can see how it's supposed to be.

How might you be living in slavery in some areas of your life? Do you have a hard time accepting God's forgiveness when you make a mistake? Do you have a difficult time forgiving others?

How is your life teaching your daughter about God's grace and the freedom it brings?

Daughter

> **It is for freedom that Christ has set us free. Stand firm, then, and do not let yourselves be burdened again by a yoke of slavery.**
>
> *Galatians 5:1*

How do you feel when you make a mistake?

Are you someone who calmly says, "Oh well. Whoops. I'll do better next time." Or are you someone who has a harder time letting that mistake go? Do you replay it over and over in your head—sometimes changing the decision you made or stopping yourself before you say or do the thing you wish you hadn't? Do you have a hard time forgiving yourself? Do you sulk and stew and feel horrible about yourself? Is it hard for you to feel light and happy for a while? Do you wake up under a cloud caused by your old mistake?

Sometimes we can get so caught up in trying to be perfect that we forget that with God we are always good enough. God knows we are going to mess up; in fact, He knows we are about to mess up even before we mess up! He expects us to need His help. That is why, when we come to Him and confess our sins, He recognizes when we are truly sorry and forgives us immediately. Sometimes there are things we need to do to clean up our mess if we've hurt someone (apologize, fix something), but we are right with God right away. Sadly, it can sometimes take much longer for us to feel right with ourselves.

This is not what God intended at all! He wants us to be forgiven for our sins, learn from them, try not to repeat them, and move on! He wants us to let it go and let Him handle things. This verse is a good one to remember if you are a person who thinks she needs to punish herself: "It is for freedom that Christ has set us free." Tell yourself that if you are struggling with a mistake. Jesus died for our sins so that we would be free of that yuck. If we still go around, after confessing, with our heads hanging down, a frown on our face, still upset, it means that we have not truly accepted God's grace. What a waste of a beautiful gift! Jesus wants you to experience the freedom that He died to give you.

This verse also says, "Do not let yourselves be burdened again by a yoke of slavery." Slavery can be the weight of old sins. Slavery can be other people's opinions. Slavery means living your life in darkness—without the light of God's love.

And that, my dear, is not the life for you.

Think about the way you treat yourself when you make a mistake. Are you quick to confess your sin, or are you so ashamed that you try to hide it? Once you confess, do you believe that God truly has taken that sin and made your heart clean? This week I want you to practice letting go and moving on—for freedom's sake. And yours.

Mother

> A person may think their own ways are right, but
> the LORD weighs the heart.
>
> *Proverbs 21:2*

I have an old convertible Volkswagen Beetle at our house in California. And when I'm on Highway 101 and trying to change lanes, I am often met with honks and squealing brakes, followed by angry glares and shaking fists. I am not on my phone—that's illegal in California anyway. I am not texting. I am not turning around to talk to my girls in the backseat. I really am paying attention. It's just that a convertible top has a serious blind spot, just about the length of a car. I'm not kidding; try to drive one and you will see exactly what I mean.

I'm as surprised by the honking as the other driver was by almost being cut off. And I've learned over the years that I don't have blind spots only when I'm driving. I have plenty of blind spots in general about myself. And so do you. We all do. There are things we would rather not see, and other things that we legitimately are unaware of but are as obvious to other people as a car in the road. When I'm feeling fit and trim, I don't mind getting on the scale. When I feel bloated and gross, no way am I stepping on that thing. I don't want to know what I don't want to know—right? The thing is, that's usually when I really need to know, so I can do something about it before it becomes a bigger problem.

We need God's help. We need to ask God to give us eyes to see ourselves the way He sees us. Sometimes this helps us view ourselves much more kindly. Other times we need to see ourselves much more accurately—and this isn't always pretty. Me: *Hey God, how do I look to You today?* God: *Actually, Kristin, I'm glad you asked. You are looking particularly selfish today.* Wow. Ouch. But ultimately very helpful. You can't change what you can't (or won't) see.

Sometimes the clearest perspective of ourselves comes from other people. It can come from our children, who really see us, warts and all. Or it can come from our spouse, or our close friends and family members—they have the intimacy with us to know our heart and the proximity to see us often, and from many angles. If we are lucky, we also have the kind of relationship where they can speak the truth to us (with love), and we can handle it.

This week, pick an area of struggle for you where you are looking to grow. Pray to God or ask a close and trusted confidante to help you see your part in the situation. Ask her to be bold in her honesty. Pray for your defensive spirit to remain on the sidelines. Listen carefully and openly. Don't shoot the messenger; thank her. This is exactly what you need to begin to address your blind spots.

With God's help, we can change what we are willing to see.

Daughter

> **A person may think their own ways are right, but the LORD weighs the heart.**
>
> **Proverbs 21:2**

My daughter Isabelle and I had an argument one day. She wanted to do something with her friend, and I didn't really want her to go. She kept bugging me, and finally I just said, "*Fine*, go. Do it. Whatever." Not very mature, I know, but I said that.

Isabelle looked at me for a minute, like she was weighing whether or not to speak her mind, and finally she said, "That's it! That's the thing you do that I just can't stand! You say one thing but you really mean another. I can tell you're mad or disappointed, but you won't tell the truth. I really don't like you when you do that!" She was really worked up.

I had half a mind to be mad right back at her, but I couldn't. *Because she was telling the truth.*

As hard as it was to admit it, I needed her to point out something I was doing that I cannot stand in other people—and I really cannot stand it in myself. "Isabelle," I told her, "that thing you are talking about is called passive-aggressive. It's saying one thing but really meaning another. It's mean and rude, and I don't want to be like that, ever. To you or anyone else. Thank you for telling me, and I want you to let me know whenever you see that in me again so I can fix it." It hurt, but I meant it. I want to know when I'm acting ugly or when I'm wrong. If I can't see it, and no one points it out to me, how on earth can I ever fix it?

The things we can't see about ourselves are sometimes referred to as blind spots. It's a good habit to ask God to reveal your blind spots to you. You can also ask trusted friends or family members to help you see yourself more clearly, especially if you are struggling in a certain area and are unable to see your part in the situation. Hearing the truth isn't always easy, but if it's spoken with love, it always heals more than it hurts. Don't be afraid to ask.

A prayer for you this week:

Lord, I can't always see myself clearly. But You can, and You do. Reveal myself to me. Show me the things You want me to work on, the areas where You want me to change and grow. Help me to listen and accept when someone loving and godly has something to say to me that I really need to hear. If it's a message from You, let me hear it and teach me how to do something about it. You see my heart, Lord, and I want it to be beautiful. In Jesus' name, amen.

Mother

> We hear that some among you are idle and disruptive. They are not busy; they are busybodies. Such people we command and urge in the Lord Jesus Christ to settle down and earn the food they eat. And as for you, brothers and sisters, never tire of doing what is good.
>
> *2 Thessalonians 3:11–13*

Every generation has probably noted that the upcoming generation does not work as hard, is more entitled, and is less motivated. In our culture of comfort, it's a constant battle to keep our kids humble, inspired, and working hard. Obesity is a bigger problem than ever before in history. Kids are sitting around in front of screens all day, unlike any generation before. With social media so pervasive, people are more up in each other's business than they are up and at 'em.

Idleness and entitlement go hand in hand. We have to teach our daughters how to combat idleness, how to go after their goals rather than waiting for their ship to come in. If we encourage or even require each person in our household to pull his or her own weight, our kids will be better prepared to make a contribution in the world. The problem is, in an effort to love or compensate for a lack of time, we often do things for our children that they should be doing for themselves.

I know plenty of grown women whom I consider to be idle, plenty of women who are more busybodies than they are busy making it happen. They are often uninteresting, and their children are often spoiled. They can look forward to doing laundry for their thirty-year-old child who lives at home. We have to be strong if we expect our daughters to grow up stronger. Our girls have to see us working hard if they will ever value hard work. We need to make an effort to earn the food we eat, and think and dream big. Financial comfort is not a pass to be idle, just as financial need is not a pass to be striving and unbalanced. We need to live meaningful, purposeful, productive lives. Our children need to know we value and prioritize them, but they also need to know we have a life outside of them and our own unique role in God's Kingdom. If we make our lives all about our children, then they will naturally assume the world revolves around them. It's not their fault—it's ours.

We have to grow in order to help our daughters grow up.

Do these words make you want to cringe or shout amen? Although harsh, this passage is boot camp for the idle soul. We cannot criticize in others what we model ourselves. Are you setting the example of a balanced, purposeful life for your daughter? Are you modeling a life that is not selfish, idle, or indulgent? Are you willing to press on, persevere, and lead by example?

Daughter

> We hear that some among you are idle and disruptive. They are not busy; they are busybodies. Such people we command and urge in the Lord Jesus Christ to settle down and earn the food they eat. And as for you, brothers and sisters, never tire of doing what is good.
>
> *2 Thessalonians 3:11–13*

Do you have a comfortable life? If you have something to eat, clean water to drink, a bed to sleep in, a family to love you, and a school and church to attend, you are one of the luckiest girls in the whole world.

Because we have such comfortable lives, it's easy to take things for granted. Food just appears in the refrigerator. We have clothes that get clean. We assume certain things will be done for us, simply because that's the way it has always been. This Scripture sheds some light into our comfortable lives. God does not consider comfort an excuse to be idle or lazy. He wants each one of us to carry our load, to do the work that is ours to do.

Even if no one in your family outlines specific jobs for you, think about ways you can contribute to your household. Can you do chores without being asked or without expecting to be handed an allowance? Do you work hard at your job, which is being a student? Do you go the extra mile and make the best grades you can? Do you take good care of your body, with sleep, healthy food, water, and regular exercise? Do you help out at mealtimes, or do you expect to be served? Do you clean up after yourself? Do you remember your manners? Do you make an effort to earn some spending money, or do you wait for a handout? Are you grateful for your blessings?

A busybody is someone who pays more attention to what other people are doing than what needs to be done. Don't be a busybody. Instead, get busy sharing your time and talents.

Do you want to take a stand against idleness? This week take a break from screens and see what you can do with the time you have.

Think about what you might want to do or be in the future and consider what steps you can take in that direction today.

You are not too young to make a difference. You are not too young to make your own amazing life.

Mother

Blessed is the one you discipline, LORD, the one you teach from your law.

Psalm 94:12

I don't like using my bossy mama voice. I don't like being stern and enforcing consequences. I don't like revoking privileges. I don't like intervening in sibling warfare. I don't like the word "no" half as much as I like the word "yes." I don't like pulling my kids aside to reinforce proper manners or acceptable behavior. It's exhausting. It's repetitive.

Proper discipline has to come from authority figures (God, Mom, Dad, extended family, parents of friends, teachers, coaches, clergy) before there is any hope for it to become self-discipline. We have to set clear limits and outline clear expectations about what is okay and not okay in our family. It doesn't always look like other families, and that has to be respected. Sometimes we get stuck in a situation and genuinely don't know which way to go, and at that time we need to seek God's wisdom together, through God's Word or wise counsel. It's okay to not know what to do, but our girls need to see us seeking first instead of forging ahead blindly.

Our character, and the character of our daughters, is

formed by doing the right thing consistently over time, whether we feel like it or not, whether anyone is watching us or not. Ultimately discipline can't be about pleasing Mom because there comes a point (sooner than we'd like) where we can't watch our girls all the time, or even most of the time. At this point, striving for good character has to be a matter of pleasing God, and the choices a child makes about the kind of person she wants to become. The responsibility for creating this foundation of discipline rests on our meager shoulders. We can bear up under the responsibility or be crushed later by our lack of fortitude.

Our daughters' eyes are on us all the time. They look for instruction, they look for example, they look for cues, they look for affirmation, and they look for correction. If our words of discipline are not in harmony with our own actions, we lose our audience. And our daughters risk losing their way.

Are you living a life that exemplifies good character? Are your words and your actions in alignment with your heart, and with God's best? This week, be extra diligent about your words and decisions, thinking each time that your daughter is watching, whether she is or not. Explain to her how you struggle sometimes to do the right thing, so she will feel more open to sharing her struggles with you.

Look for areas of your life that are in need of discipline, and see where you can tighten things up.

Daughter

> **Blessed is the one you discipline, LORD, the one you teach from your law.**
>
> **Psalm 94:12**

It doesn't feel good to be disciplined. When we get corrected or suffer consequences for our poor choices, we might feel sad, angry, frustrated, or ashamed. Because discipline doesn't necessarily feel good, we mistakenly might view it as a bad thing. Just like getting shots at the doctor's office doesn't feel good and we don't like them, they are something we have to do for our own good. A quick shot is far better than one day getting a horrible disease that could kill you. But at the time you get the shot, it feels like the worst thing in the world.

Discipline is kind of like that shot. We take a little pain now in order to avoid something horrible down the road. If your parents, teachers, or coaches didn't correct you and enforce consequences now, you would grow up into a mess of a person. Discipline is what helps build the character you will need to grow up into someone with strong values. This is the time in your life when you are learning how to make good choices. And we learn this when we sometimes make bad choices and have to suffer the consequences, otherwise how would we ever know the difference?

Your parents and teachers discipline you for the same reason that God disciplines all His people: discipline is a sign of love. If you didn't love someone, you wouldn't care at all about how they turned out—they could grow up to be totally selfish, friendless, sick, miserable, or in jail and you couldn't care less. But loving someone means teaching them and helping them grow into the great person that God created them to be.

Discipline is a blessing, just as this verse from Psalm 94 says. It is a sign that someone sees something good in you and wants to help you shine. Eventually, if you learn everything you can from discipline early on, with God's help you will be able to discipline yourself. You will know right from wrong because someone loved you enough to teach you.

This week, when someone corrects your behavior, remember that they correct you because they care. Discipline is not mean (it shouldn't be, anyway); it is a natural consequence of a choice you made. Try your best to think before you act.

Find opportunities to discipline yourself before anyone has to say a word. You know more than you think you do. You can do the right thing.

Mother

> I do not understand what I do. For what I want to
> do I do not do, but what I hate I do.
>
> *Romans 7:15*

If you have ever plummeted into a pit of sin, this verse can give you chills. The day you discover that you are just as capable of horrible things as you considered "other people" to be is a sad and sobering day. But it's also a revelation and a brand-new way to experience God's mercy and His amazing, unfathomable grace. You won't ever look at sin, or sinners, the same way again. When prideful onlookers chide, "How could she?!" you will know exactly how she could, and instead of judging, you will be able to comfort and correct. Sin personalizes the Christian faith because we realize that when Jesus died to free people from sin, He meant us. You. Me. Our sin. From the dank and dreary vista of the pit, we realize just how undeserving we are of His forgiveness. That is the seed of compassion that will enable us to be a forgiving person for the rest of our lives. Think about it: If you think you never make mistakes, how will you tolerate mistakes in others? Pride comes before a fall, y'all.

If you haven't come face-to-face with your own depravity yet, you will. Sorry, but it's true. Not one of us is without sin—even Paul! And after his conversion, he was one of God's finest. Even he did not understand himself and his contradictory nature. We want to be good and do what's right, but we are *broken people*. Without the constant intervention of the Holy Spirit, we are selfish, sneaky, and lustful. To pretend otherwise is to hide and rationalize. Better to face the truth, get on our knees, and start fresh every day.

We can't correct what we won't admit. At the first sign of temptation, it's crucial that we go to God. Sometimes this means we have to go to a trusted brother or sister in faith and put our yuck out in the open. Only the light of God can fry the seed of sin. If we keep it in the dark, it grows—fast.

We have to be open with our daughters about our own brokenness. If we don't admit our struggles with sin, they will think they should be ashamed of theirs. We can't help them if they won't talk to us. No one wants to share something ugly with someone who pretends to be perfect. A message of vulnerability and victory is a testament to the saving power of God. Share your message.

Do you try to present a perfect picture to your daughter? Are you open to hearing the truth—about yourself and others—whether good or bad? Share a struggle with your daughter this week and allow God's lesson to teach you both. Let your vulnerability invite hers, and cultivate the kind of communication that heals.

Daughter

> I do not understand what I do. For what I want to do I do not do, but what I hate I do.
>
> **Romans 7:15**

Do you ever feel like a mystery, even to yourself? Is it sometimes hard to understand your own moods, your reactions to things, your choices? Sometimes we know exactly what we should do, and yet we do exactly the opposite.

One of my daughters has a pretty short fuse. She has to work hard to keep it together when she's in a bad mood or someone is pushing her buttons. We have talked many times about how important it is for her to get some space in those situations. When her fuse is short, she has to take time to cool off so she can calmly decide what to say and do. If she doesn't do this, there is a very good chance that instead of deciding, she will just explode.

Now she knows the right thing to do, and she knows how to take care of herself in those situations. And most of the time, she does just fine. But there are those other times, maybe when she is tired or in an extra bad mood, when she reacts without thinking. She does the very thing that she doesn't want to do. I know this frustrates her just as much as it frustrates everyone else.

I try to explain to her that this frustration is not just because she is young—people of all ages experience the same problem. People are not perfect; that's just the way it is. We do the best we can, which looks different on different days, but it is our imperfection and our mistakes that remind us of how much we need God. The gift of His forgiveness, and what He did for us on the cross, would seem meaningless if we didn't think we needed it.

Try your best, of course, but don't be so hard on yourself when you make mistakes. If the holy people in the Bible sinned and were forgiven, then surely it's okay if we mess up too. God loves us, just the way we are, no matter what. He understands that we sometimes do the exact thing that we didn't want to do.

With His help, we can try to do better next time. Be patient with yourself.

This week, talk to your mom about sin. Tell her about things you struggle with and ask her to tell you about hers. Sometimes just getting it off your chest can make a big difference. When you feel tempted or you feel a bad decision coming, take a time-out and get some space. Ask God to point you in the right direction.

Mother

> Do not be anxious about anything, but in every situation, by prayer and petition, with thanksgiving, present your requests to God. And the peace of God, which transcends all understanding, will guard your hearts and your minds in Christ Jesus.
>
> *Philippians 4:6–7*

When I was growing up, any time I told my mom to stop worrying, she would reply, "I'm a mom, that's just what I do." I never understood that until I had children of my own and learned the real meaning of worry. When I got divorced, my kids were ages three, one, and one. Every time they left my house, I worried, not because I didn't trust their dad to take care of them, but simply because I wasn't there. Besides, worrying gave me something specific and consuming to do while I pieced my life back together. But worry, as we all know, is pointless.

Being careful and diligent in order to prevent potential problems is useful. Doing the best we can in any given situation is a good plan. But letting our minds spin out of control with all the things that could or might happen—well, that's just an impossible way to live.

Not only that, but worry is a sin. Worry is prideful. Worry is the equivalent of telling God that you know more than He does and can take care of people and situations better than He can. To add insult to injury, worrying is a great way to show God just how much you don't trust Him. The only antidote for worry is faith. When we are overcome with anxiety, the best path to peace is to first repent of the sin of worry and restate our belief. A simple "I trust you, Jesus" can quiet an uneasy and noisy mind. And then we turn all our concerns over to God in prayer. We ask Him to intervene and intercede, and we thank Him in advance. And then, perhaps hardest of all, we release the matter into His capable hands. We leave it there and go on with our day, letting God's peace guard our heart and mind.

I am having some luck working through this process, up until the part where I have to release it and go about my day. I get stuck there. Maybe you can relate? I vent all my worries to God, leaving my burdens in the right place, only later to feel like I want to go back and pick them up. Perhaps worrying gives control freaks a sense of purpose; I'm not sure. All I know is that I desperately want the kind of peace that transcends all understanding. I have felt it on enough occasions to believe that it exists and is available for open-hearted seekers everywhere. It's worth the quest.

Are you taking all of your requests to God, or do you prefer to worry over them personally? Think honestly about any positive change that was achieved through worry. Let me help you: none. Now consider positive changes that were achieved through prayer. You can see where this is going. Your challenge this week is to be mindful of your wandering mind and begin to turn worry into faith.

Daughter

> Do not be anxious about anything, but in every situation, by prayer and petition, with thanksgiving, present your requests to God. And the peace of God, which transcends all understanding, will guard your hearts and your minds in Christ Jesus.
>
> *Philippians 4:6–7*

Are you a worrier? Do you worry about tests, performances, your appearance, tryouts, relationships, health, sports, your family, or uncomfortable conversations? Do you worry about the future, things you can't see, can't prevent, and couldn't change anyway, even if you knew they were coming?

There are some people who are totally carefree, but they are rare.

Most of us fall somewhere in the middle of those who rarely worry and those who worry a lot. It's just part of human nature to think that we can change things or stop things from happening simply by going over and over them in our minds. Worry is not a form of prevention—worry is a form of sin! When we worry it is just like telling God we don't trust Him to take care of us. Can you imagine how that must make Him feel? God loves His children, wants the best for us all, and wants to take care of us. Most of all He wants the kind of loving relationship that grows from trust. He wants us to bring our problems and our needs to Him and trust Him to solve things for us in the way that only He can. God can open doors for us and provide new solutions in ways that we can't even see. But in order to fully realize what He is doing for us, we have to change our worry into faith.

The first thing to do when you feel anxious or worried is to *stop* what you're doing. You need time to get calm and connect with God. Step 2 is to repent of the sin of worry and tell God that you trust Him to take care of you. Perhaps speak it out loud so you can remind yourself at the same time. *Jesus, I trust You.* Next, pray about whatever is bothering you, whatever is clouding your mind. Tell Him what you need and thank Him in advance for His help. Then, after having told Him all about it, leave the situation in His mighty hands. Finally, move on and trust that He knows what He's doing (because He does).

The result of releasing anxiety to God is total peace or, as this verse describes, the kind of peace that makes no sense, peace so complete that we can hardly understand it. This is the kind of peace we cannot reach on our own, so there is only one way to explain it: it has to come from God. When our problems get worked out in such a miraculous way, we know it has to come from God. When we feel steady even before things are any better, we know that feeling comes from God.

Note any time this week that you feel worried or anxious. Are you trying to control or fix things on your own? God wants to take your problems and give you peace in return. Will you let Him?

Mother

> What good is it, my brothers and sisters, if some-
> one claims to have faith but has no deeds? Can
> such faith save them?
>
> *James 2:14*

Faith without deeds is like a covered lamp (see Mt 5:14–16). The light is there, but no one is able to see it. No paths are illuminated. No lost people are found. No frightened people are comforted. No lonely or broken people are revealed and restored. The world desperately needs to see the light of faith that illuminates from every believer! It does matter what goes on in the privacy of our own hearts—God sees everything and He knows if we believe. But when our faith stops there and stays locked inside, we are not allowing our faith to help and heal others. When you have something so special, it's selfish to be unwilling to share it.

This does not mean that everyone is called to be a minister or priest, or to stand on the street corner with signs and preach the gospel, or to go on mission trips to far-away lands, or to write books or teach classes about faith. Not everyone is called to share faith in a public way. Some people share faith in more intimate ways, and this is just as powerful and meaningful. A wonderful woman named Suzanne has done my hair for many years, and I guarantee you that everyone who sits in her chair is affected by her faith. Maybe it's the way she really listens to her clients. Maybe it's the biblically sound advice she offers, or the promise to pray, or the way she always manages to bring the conversation back to God. She is always ministering.

Every interaction we have with people is an opportunity to share faith. Even when the conversation is about ordinary things, the perspective of a believer is anything but ordinary. When we live our lives peacefully, joyfully, gratefully, regardless of circumstances, people begin to wonder about the cause for the hope we have. People see something different, something they can't quite put a finger on, and something they definitely want. Over time they may even be so bold as to ask, which may be in the form of a question like, "How do you do it?" That is a perfect chance, teed up by God Himself, to smile and respond: "Oh, I don't do it at all. God does."

See where the opportunities take you. Be open. Share the reason behind the hope you have. Let your light shine, especially in front of your daughter.

Do you let your faith shine, or do you have a tendency to keep it dim? What are you afraid of? This week keep your eyes open for an opportunity to go out of your way to do something different. Listen to someone. Do something kind. Match your faith with works and share God's love with the world.

Daughter

> **What good is it, my brothers and sisters, if some-one claims to have faith but has no deeds? Can such faith save them?**
>
> *James 2:14*

For some people, faith is a very private thing. It may be that way for you, and that's okay.

Some people don't talk much about what they believe; they prefer to have a relationship with God that involves quiet, personal prayers. They may not be comfortable doing Bible studies or going to Young Life or doing anything that labels them as a Christian.

This verse isn't talking about God-related activities. It's talking about what overflows from a heart that is close to God. When you believe God, your relationship with Him deepens, and your faith grows. When your faith grows, you change. You can't help it. It just happens.

When you feel loved by God, you feel differently about yourself, which causes you to think different thoughts, which causes you to do things differently. This is what the verse from James means about deeds. Deeds are your actions—the way you treat people, and the way you return God's love to the world. When God loves you, your heart fills all the way up, so full that some of that love will spill out.

This extra love may mean that you will be able to notice people who feel sad or left out and try to include them. Or perhaps you will be able to be more patient with your brother, sister, parent, or friend. You may feel like donating some of your old toys and clothes to people in need. Or you might have a new attitude when people say mean things about someone else. God's overflowing love changes people. When you are loved in such a complete way, it makes it easier to love other people—even people you don't know or don't like.

People may notice something different about you because your heart is so full. They may feel drawn to you or want to be around you and not even understand the real reason you sparkle.

Faith and deeds go together, not because you owe God your goodness, but because you love Him and He loves you so much you can't help being loving.

This week, spend time in prayer, asking God to fill your heart to the point that it overflows. Realize how that feels. How does it change the way you look at other people or go about your day? Do you feel kind deeds happen more naturally when you take time to experience God's kindness and generosity toward you?

Mother

> Then the man said, "Your name will no longer be Jacob, but Israel..."
>
> *Genesis 32:28*

Do you remember the story? Jacob wrestled with a man all night long, whom he later discovered to be God. Jacob refused to quit until he had received a blessing, and, finally, after a full night's struggle, his blessing was granted.

I love what this story suggests about our struggles.

Fortitude...perseverance...endurance...they matter deeply. There are times when we struggle against difficult people or difficult circumstances; you can probably pick out memories like that quite easily. Or perhaps you are in the midst of that kind of struggle now. Wrestling with God, however, is a different kind of struggle.

It reminds me of when my children were very young and having a tantrum. How sometimes, in order to calm them, I had to literally wrap myself around them to soothe them. They flailed at first, but relief eventually overpowered their frustration and they relaxed gratefully into me. They never had a chance to truly overpower me (now would be a different story!), yet fighting me and feeling my strength was the thing that finally made everything okay. Today when my kids fight me, it's not physical anymore, but mental and emotional, as they push against my limits and boundaries, testing them, wanting to know that the limits—and the woman who makes them—are solid. It's a relief to them, even if they would never admit it!

We are God's children, and we wrestle Him in similar ways and for similar reasons. I have gone to the mat with God on several occasions, trying to maintain that I can do things my way instead of His. Or that I can resist the ways that He intends to shape my character. It's laughable, really, to think that I go to the mat to wrestle with God. I struggle and squirm, and, finally, when I have worn myself out completely, He simply holds me and I am His. Think of Jacob's wrestling match the next time you find yourself on the mat. Some people quit too soon, and they feel the pain of hard times but never push through to the finish. They miss the refinement. They miss the deeper lesson. They miss the transformation. They miss the comfort. They miss the blessing.

Jacob was so transformed by his struggles that he had to be renamed! He just wasn't the same guy anymore. We can be new people through our struggles as well.

Don't quit too soon. Hang in there.

Are you in the midst of something right now? Are you fighting God, resisting Him as He tries to change you in a certain way? Look for the lesson behind your struggle and learn everything you possibly can. Make the pain worthwhile.

Daughter

> **Then the man said, "Your name will no longer be Jacob, but Israel..."**
>
> *Genesis 32:28*

This story from the Bible is about a man named Jacob who was wrestling all night, fighting against a strong man he later learned was actually not a man at all, but God Himself.

There are times when we wrestle with God too. Maybe we don't wrestle literally, in a physical way, but we definitely wrestle in a spiritual way. Sometimes when God wants to change us, or mold our character to be more like His, we resist Him because His lessons aren't always easy or comfortable. We think that it's fine just to stay the way we are, even if God has bigger and better plans for us. So we resist Him, and He presses on, and this leads to a spiritual wrestling match.

It's kind of funny because anyone who tries to wrestle the most powerful force in the universe with wimpy human strength will always lose, right? But God is patient with us when we fight Him. Just like your mom is patient with you (or tries to be) when you fight her rules and limits. Your mom knows that sometimes you have to do some things for your own good, whether you like it or not. And God knows that about everyone—kids and grown-ups. We all wrestle and resist, and we all eventually realize that He is in control and He knows best, and He wants what's best for us because He loves us.

In the Bible story, Jacob refused to stop wrestling until God blessed him. Finally, after a long night of struggle, God blessed Him. And Jacob was so changed by the struggle and the blessing that he even needed a new name! That's how much God can change us when we go through a challenge with Him. But the thing is, we can't give up. We can't close our hearts and minds and be unwilling to grow. It's the hard stuff, the struggles, that make us grow, not the easy times. But we don't want to give up before we make it all the way through with God. We don't want to miss the blessing.

Can you think of a hard time or situation when you felt like giving up? How did you feel after you overcame the challenge? What do you think God's lesson was for you in that experience? How did you grow? Are you stronger because of it? Is your faith stronger too?

If so, then you did not miss your blessing!

Mother

> "No one will be able to stand against you all the days of your life. As I was with Moses, so I will be with you; I will never leave you nor forsake you."
>
> *Joshua 1:5*

Read this verse out loud and let the words sink in, as spoken directly from God to you.

By the time we are adults, we have all experienced some kind of loss, hurt, betrayal, or abandonment. It's a wound inside our hearts that, left unhealed, can infect our future relationships. But when we take this verse to heart and apply it like a balm to any wound of past hurts, true healing begins. When we recognize and believe that God won't leave us, we finally understand that we will be okay if someone else does. We can stop fearing, stop clutching, and start being free.

God is with us, close enough that we can lean on Him. We can pass Him the weight of our sorrows and disappointments, and His strength can offset the weariness of our days. When we believe that He is always beside us, we can be healed of the fear that we are not enough. "What if I can't?" is transformed into a peaceful shrug and the notion that maybe *I* can't, but *we* can. That is the beginning of unshakeable confidence. Not puny and not prideful—simply solid.

Do you understand that God promises that no one will be able to stand against you? In today's language He is saying, "I always have your back. Always." This means we can let go of the fear of being hurt. Because if He doesn't prevent the hurt, He will always soothe it, and in that case, what's to worry about? It will all be okay.

Did you hear that?

It will all be okay.

God wants you to know that. He tells us over and over again in His Word. Do not be afraid. Do not be discouraged. I won't leave you. I won't forsake you. I have a plan for you, a future and a hope. Be strong and courageous. Exchange yokes with me. My burden is easy and light. Peace be with you.

When you read this verse out loud, is it difficult for you to comprehend that these promises are meant for you? How does it change your heart and your life to believe them, to believe Him?

What wounds do you need to heal? Can you use this verse or seek others to apply directly to past hurts? Speaking God's truth over old pain yields new freedom. It's never too late to be free. Free mothers have a far better chance of raising free daughters.

Daughter

> "No one will be able to stand against you all the days of your life. As I was with Moses, so I will be with you; I will never leave you nor forsake you."
> *Joshua 1:5*

Life involves a certain amount of leaving. Some of it is a normal part of growing, and some of it simply hurts.

Sometimes friends leave us; they move away or move on. We leave certain schools and go to others. Sometimes our parents divorce and we go back and forth between houses, always leaving someone. We leave a favorite teacher at the end of the year, or a favorite coach at the end of a season. Sometimes our priest or pastor leaves our church and goes to another one. When you're older and dating, you will leave several people, or they will leave you, before you meet your husband.

We can be certain of two things. First, life here on earth is uncertain. And second, God is certain, and He promises never to leave us.

Isn't that a beautiful and comforting thought? No matter where we are or what is happening to us, God will be by our side and see us through. When we understand that fact and believe God's promise, we are able to love people in a healthy way. We don't have to cling to them or be afraid of being alone if they go because we will never truly be alone. We can be confident and free, knowing we can love and let go, because we have the ultimate safety net at all times—God's loving arms.

This verse speaks about the promise of God's continued protection and His continued presence. He always has your back, all the days of your life.

Do you ever feel alone or left out? What do you do with those feelings?

Next time you feel that way, take those feelings to God in prayer. Let Him remind you that you are His and He is not going anywhere without you. Practice saying this verse out loud, and try to let God's promises soak deep into your heart.

How does knowing you will never really be left alone change the way you might act in some of your friendships? Do you clutch tightly to your friends or parents in a fearful way, or do you feel free and safe to love people and give them space?

Mother

> **"Still other seed fell on good soil. It came up and yielded a crop, a hundred times more than was sown."** . . .
>
> *Luke 8:8*

In this simple parable about the farmer scattering seed, Jesus offers some of the most profound teaching about motherhood.

Go to your Bible and check out Luke 8:4–8. If Jesus is the farmer scattering seeds of truth for our children, our job as mothers is to make sure that the soil of their heart is a well-prepared field.

If we don't help them prepare their hearts for faith, they will be like the trampled path, the rock, or the thorns. The seeds of faith will be stepped on, withered, malnourished, or choked by the weeds of the world. Their faith will never grow because the conditions in their hearts are unsuitable over time. Tilling this field starts when our girls are young. We help them work the soil of their hearts until they are old enough and experienced enough to take over their own gardens.

It isn't enough to let other people assume this responsibility—their church, their school, their Bible study leader. This is not something that will happen by default. In fact, the brokenness of the world opposes conditions needed for good soil. It is not okay to tend to other aspects of raising a child and yet leave their spiritual development to chance or in the hands of others. A girl needs to learn certain things from her mother.

Spend some time this week assessing the condition of your own garden. How is your heart? If your field is trampled, rocky, or filled with weeds, chances are the seeds of God's teaching are not taking root. This learning process is lifelong after all. We are learning alongside our daughters, and by maintaining our good soil, we are better equipped to help them tend to theirs.

Are you taking responsibility for your daughter's spiritual development or leaving it primarily in the hands of others?

How can you make the gardening of a heart a fun and fruitful process with your daughter?

How are the seeds of God's teaching faring in your soil?

What weeds threaten to choke what has been planted in your garden? (Bitterness? Unforgiveness? Unconfessed sin? Rationalization? Busyness? Pride?) This week, get on your knees and start pulling weeds.

Daughter

> **"Still other seed fell on good soil. It came up and yielded a crop, a hundred times more than was sown."** ...
>
> *Luke 8:8*

This verse comes from the Parable of the Sower. Parables are stories, and Jesus used them a lot to explain complicated things about faith in simple ways that all people could understand. The parables are recorded in the Gospels, and we need them as much today as people did two thousand years ago.

The Parable of the Sower is a story about a farmer (the farmer represents Jesus) who is in a field scattering seeds. The seeds represent the Word of God. Jesus scatters God's Word onto the world, and different people respond differently. In the parable, some seeds land on the path and get trampled and eaten by birds. This represents people who hear God's Word, but it has no effect on their lives at all; they go on without it.

Some seeds land on the rocks, where they can't grow very deep roots, so they soon die. These are like the people who hear the messages from God and are excited at first, but give up on God as soon as they have a problem or get busy with other things.

Some seeds land in the weeds and thorns and are choked out. These are like the people who commit to their faith, but eventually the worries and temptations of life cause their faith to die.

Finally, some seeds land in good soil. This is soil that isn't trampled, rocky, or full of weeds. This is like the garden in the hearts of people who really love Jesus and keep their commitment to follow Him, no matter what. The seeds of God's Word grow long roots in the good soil, and their faith grows and grows—for the rest of their lives.

You can create good soil in your heart. Ask Jesus to help you prepare your garden so that there are no rocks or weeds to get in the way of your faith. Solid roots of faith are developed by prayer, by reading your Bible, by going to church and Bible studies, and by being mindful of the things and people that you allow in your garden.

Are you someone who wants to have good soil?

How can you better prepare the soil of your heart this week so that the seeds of God's Word can start growing deep roots in you?

Mother

> "...First take the plank out of your own eye, and then you will see clearly to remove the speck from your brother's eye."
>
> *Matthew 7:5*

Pride and judgment: such an unhappy couple, yet they always seem to be attracted to one another.

It's quite easy to recognize the faults, shortcomings, annoying habits, and sins of someone else. If we aren't in a good place, it's easy to feel provoked, irritated, and judgmental of other people. Every time we focus our attention on someone else's character flaws it provides a welcome respite from looking in the mirror and seeing the work we need to do on ourselves. Our pride becomes a deflector, shining light on other people's weak spots so we can rationalize our own. *Well, at least I don't do that, or have that problem...*

I have a friend who, during Lent, stopped herself every single time she was bugged by someone else. She paused and prayed and asked God to reveal the sin within her that caused her to be so annoyed by someone else. Sometimes she discovered that she was so provoked by their behavior because she was repulsed by the same exact trait in herself. Other times she uncovered a "sister sin" in herself, something equally ugly but different, that was reacting to the ugliness in someone else. That spring, she learned powerful lessons about her tendency to judge and her willingness to work on the one thing she could change (with God's help): herself.

Her work inspired me to take a look at my own tendencies to judge and my reasons behind them—my pride, my selfishness, my blind spots, my laziness, my lack of faith, and my fear. It isn't pretty to see what lurks behind personal righteousness. But in the process of removing planks, our vision is restored. And with fresh eyes, we may find that we are more interested in looking at what God wants to show us and teach us than we are at looking at other people's specks.

Maybe you carry a compact or a small mirror in your purse. Or maybe you drive a lot so you can use the rearview mirror in your car. Whatever you choose, find a touch point to remind you of this verse. This week, whenever you feel your spirit of judgment ignite, look in the mirror and turn your gaze back on yourself. Look for your own plank and, with it, the lesson that God is implying. Little by little you will discover less judgment and more healing. This sets you free to respond to others with love and compassion, which pleases our Father. Judgmental mothers raise judgmental girls, so let's get clearer vision on the legacy we want to leave.

Lord, help me this week to pay more attention to my own work than to what others should be doing. Help me to see myself clearly and cooperate with You to heal whatever clouds my vision. In Jesus' name, amen.

Daughter

> "...First take the plank out of your own eye, and then you will see clearly to remove the speck from your brother's eye."
>
> *Matthew 7:5*

This verse is about judgment, but not judgment as it refers to making decisions. The word "judgment" can also mean the way we look at people and judge them, often harshly.

I know that whenever I am not in a good place, or when I don't feel particularly good about myself, I tend to be a lot harder on other people. I judge their choices and their words, and—especially if they happen to bug me—I judge them in a not-so-nice way. I think that when I'm busy judging other people or looking at their mistakes, I don't have to pay as much attention to my own. And this is far more pleasant than focusing on the things that are wrong with me, in my heart.

But God doesn't have a lot of patience for people who judge, especially people who judge others but are not willing to do their own work and make their own changes and improvements. God says that He alone is the only Judge.

Do you notice the size difference in this verse between a plank and a speck? A plank is a long piece of wood, and a speck could be a piece of dust. This verse reminds us that our own fault and our own sin needs to be viewed as a bigger problem than someone else's. This doesn't mean that our sins are worse; it means that they are more important for us to pay attention to. Why?

The only thing we can really change is ourself, so God wants us to start there. Ideally, if we are so busy doing our own work, we won't have time to pick on other people about theirs. And God wants us each to do our own work, so that we will all be growing closer to Him all the time.

Do you have certain people that just bug you? Do they have habits that annoy you or certain things that you simply cannot stand? Does being critical of them make you feel better about yourself?

If so, you have a plank-speck situation. This week is a great week to take a look at what's really going on. When something about someone else really bothers you, it is a clue that there is something about you that needs to change too. And since you can actually do something about that, why don't you?

This week, when you notice people or things that irritate you, try to look deeper and see what reflects back to you. Find your plank. Are you sometimes selfish or impatient? Are you too critical? Could you be more compassionate? Ask God to remind you of your own work and then do it.

Mother

A generous person will prosper; whoever refreshes others will be refreshed.

Proverbs 11:25

This verse propels us to do the opposite of what we feel like doing, in order to feel the way we long to feel.

Just like scarcity or the threat of it makes us want to hoard our blessings, God's Word tells us to give and we will have more. Unclenching our fists to let go and give breaks the chains that hold us back and keep us in a place of scarcity. But to give when we feel like we're losing is a very hard lesson in obedience.

This verse is about generosity and refreshment. Here God is telling us that in order to feel refreshed, we must refresh others. I don't know about you, but when my tank is on empty and I'm coasting on fumes, I don't feel like I have it in me to show up or put up for someone else. I have enough on my plate, thank you very much. But God is relentless in this lesson, and I call it the painful lesson of getting over myself. You have to submit enough to be willing to try it, and once I was so exhausted and fed up that I did just that. I simply obeyed.

I was having a hard week, feeling like I was working my tail off, was taking care of everyone, and was virtually unseen. Can you relate? But I came across this Scripture, and, desperate for refreshment, I decided to go for it. I put my to-do list aside and thought about the people I had come across earlier that day. I decided to appreciate others, the very thing I was pining for, so I called three people and thanked them each for something that had recently helped me or affected me. I told them I wanted them to know that I saw them and appreciated them.

As soon as I hung up the phone, I felt...different. I felt seen myself. I felt thankful. I felt God's pleasure. I felt refreshed.

I filled someone else's tank instead of trying to stop the leak in my own, and what do you know, my tank magically refilled. Magic, nothing—obedience was everything. I broke the spell of my own selfishness by doing something for someone else—when I least felt like it—and the moment I obeyed I was redeemed. I possessed the very thing I was finally willing to give away.

This is my love dare for you this week. When you least feel like obeying God, do it anyway. When you are too tired to offer, offer and see that you aren't tired. When you are too angry to forgive, forgive and see that you are no longer angry but free. When you are too caught up in your own problems to see the needs of others, tend to others instead of yourself and find that your own problems have meanwhile been tended to.

Some might call it karma. I call it Christ.

Daughter

A generous person will prosper; whoever refreshes others will be refreshed.

Proverbs 11:25

Sometimes in order to believe God's spiritual principles, we have to try them out for ourselves.

And sometimes this means that we have to do the one thing that we do not feel like doing. For example, when we feel like we don't have enough (money, attention, affection, material things, etc.), the last thing we want to do is give away what we have, right? But it is exactly by doing the thing we don't want to do that we actually get the thing we need. When we don't feel loved, if, instead of feeling sorry for ourselves, we do something loving for someone else, all of a sudden we feel loved.

It's the strangest, coolest thing.

I tried this for the first time one day when I really felt unappreciated. I decided that instead of pouting and whining (which was what my bad mood and I felt like doing!) I would make a point to appreciate others. So I did. I thanked three people for things I noticed about them. They were surprised in the happiest way, and two of them told me that I made their week. I felt so good because I made someone else feel good, and in the middle of all that, I forgot all about my bad mood. I felt appreciated because I had appreciated someone else.

Try this out. Do the opposite of what you feel like doing. Compliment someone else when you are having a bad day. Or do something sweet when you feel grouchy and mean. Forgive someone else when you are mad at yourself for a mistake. Thank a teacher who you think doesn't like you. Let your sibling have his or her way when all you want is your way. Share something that you feel like hoarding all to yourself. Hug your mom when you feel like ignoring her. Do the opposite of what your selfish human nature is telling you and see how God prioritizes those who prioritize others. When you get busy taking care of someone else, God is busy taking care of you.

Your bad mood lifts, your problems fade, and your heavy heart feels light once again.

Lord, help me this week to move beyond myself. Help me to take my eyes off myself all the time and see other people and their needs. Help me to trust You more and to know that You help me even more when I'm busy helping others. Bless me and make me a blessing. In Jesus' name, amen.

Mother

> **Guard the good deposit that was entrusted to you—guard it with the help of the Holy Spirit who lives in us.**
>
> *2 Timothy 1:14*

The good deposit here that Paul is describing to Timothy is the sound teachings of Jesus Christ. As we grow in our faith, deposits of wisdom, knowledge, discernment, and understanding are given to us at appropriate times. God instills His teaching in us at the moment that we are really ready to embrace it, personalize it, and persevere in it. Sometimes we don't understand something yet because we aren't ready; our circumstances have not yet aligned in such a way that we recognize our need.

Have you ever experienced the awesome feeling of reading a verse in Scripture that you have heard or read hundreds of times, but suddenly you read it or hear it again and it's brand new, crystal clear, and makes all the sense in the world, as if it were penned just for you? Those moments are absolutely precious, like a love note straight from God.

This verse from 2 Timothy reminds us that not only must we seek growth in the application of God's teaching, but also we must guard what we have already learned! The world can easily chip away at our knowledge or dilute our understanding if we do not consciously guard our hearts and minds. We must help our daughters do the same, helping them to gain new ground on their spiritual journeys while guarding the progress that has already been made. This helps prevent backsliding and venturing offtrack.

When I was almost a teenager, our priest gave a deeply impactful homily about choices and consequences as we grow up. He described how we begin life with a clean slate, and all the possibilities and options are open to us, like a long hallway lined on both sides with open doors. When we stay faithful to God's will and consistently do our best, the doors remain open to us, and we can continue to look at options as long as we like until we figure out the path best suited to us. He then went on to discuss free will and the power we have in our choices as we work with God (or against Him) to define our future through the opening and closing of doors. I remember my priest's words to this day, and still want a hallway filled with open doors for me and for my children. We will make mistakes, but thankfully the one door that never shuts is the door to God's grace.

How does your hallway look today? Have you made choices that allow for as many options and possibilities as possible? Do you regret some slamming doors? How can you use the lessons of your hallway to help your daughter guard the good deposits of sound teaching made in her?

Daughter

> **Guard the good deposit that was entrusted to you—guard it with the help of the Holy Spirit who lives in us.**
>
> *2 Timothy 1:14*

In this verse Paul is reminding his young friend Timothy to guard the lessons God has taught him and to keep that knowledge safe and secure. Our spiritual growth is like a solid wall made of bricks or stone. When we are very young, the foundation is prepared, and it must be very strong to support the blocks of knowledge that must rest on top of it in the future. The new things we learn in our faith build on the lessons we have already learned, which is why we must guard so carefully what we are building.

The Holy Spirit helps us to guard our knowledge and keep it safe from the world. But we have a responsibility to do our part. Everything you learn now when you are young will affect the choices you make as you grow. The choices get more serious the older you get, and each choice will build on other choices to eventually become you—your heart, your character, and the life you live.

You come into life with as many possibilities as there are stars in the sky. What kind of student you are, the hobbies and sports you enjoy, the friendships you have, where you will go to college, the career path you take, the kind of man you will marry, and the type of mother you will eventually be—everything is open to you. It's like a long hallway filled with open doors. The more we guard our teaching from God and stay on His path, the more open doors we have and the longer they remain open.

But when we make choices that veer away from God's best, doors in our hallway start to slam shut. Luckily for us, the one door that never closes is the door to God's grace. We will make mistakes no matter what, but ultimately girls who know their value in Christ will make more wise choices.

Learn to guard the good deposit of God's teachings that are being made in you today. Do your best to stay on course with God and make wise choices, and watch the doors continue to open for you. The doors He shuts, no man can open, and the doors He opens, no man can shut (Rv 3:8).

Can you think of ways that you can better guard the knowledge that has been entrusted to you?

You can choose friends who strengthen and support your faith. You can read the Bible, especially when you need an answer or advice. You can pray and ask for the Holy Spirit to help you guard your heart and mind. You can practice what you are learning and grow your faith through your words and actions. You can keep a faith journal, where you record things you learn and experiences you share with God.

Mother

> With the tongue we praise our Lord and Father, and with it we curse human beings, who have been made in God's likeness. Out of the same mouth come praise and cursing. My brothers and sisters, this should not be.
>
> *James 3:9–10*

My sisters, this should not be.

My Bible study did a study on the book of James, and it was one of the hardest and best things I have ever done. It's a short book, but long on lessons. Some call it the Proverbs of the New Testament. When I am in need of a quick recheck, I often open to James and let him whip me back into line.

One of the (many) hard truths in the book of James is about the taming of the tongue. He compares the tongue to a tiny rudder that can steer the whole ship. How right is that? When our words are thoughtful and led by the Spirit, our ship stays on course no matter what the weather. I can speak for myself here, but when my tongue steers my ship unchecked, it's only a matter of time before I ram into an iceberg and start sinking. Words are powerful and potent.

The words we speak to others can lift them or level them, so let's practice speaking a language of blessings. Look for the good (the God) in people and in circumstances, and proclaim that. Notice how your ship is steered by your words. Sometimes speaking out loud can cause our feelings and intentions to follow suit. This is a mighty tool. We need to speak blessings to our daughters, to other people, and even to ourselves. We cannot praise God and curse others or ourselves. So choose.

When you catch yourself speaking negatively, stop, back up, and rephrase your words. I try to help my daughters do this all the time, yet it sneaks up on me when I need to do it for myself. When we speak negatively we limit ourselves with a fixed mindset of what we can and cannot do. A growth mindset, by contrast, opens us up to possibility and potential. When something is hard, we can remind ourselves that we love a challenge. When we fail, we can remind ourselves that next time will be so much better. When we struggle, we can remember that strength is born in strife—and press on. When we use our language purposefully, we can change ourselves and our lives.

This week, take time to read the book of James, paying special attention to the taming of the tongue.

Pay closer attention to the words you use to speak to others and to yourself. Practice stopping and rephrasing if you find yourself stuck in negative thinking. Help your daughter do the same.

Daughter

> With the tongue we praise our Lord and Father, and with it we curse human beings, who have been made in God's likeness. Out of the same mouth come praise and cursing. My brothers and sisters, this should not be.
>
> *James 3:9–10*

My sisters, this should not be.

When we speak negatively, about others or about ourselves, it always leaves a bitter aftertaste in our mouths. Since God created and loves everyone, when we use words to hurt someone else (or ourselves) we are hurting God.

This week, pay attention to the words you use when you talk about other people. Think about how God would define your talk—as blessing or cursing?

I'm also going to ask you to pay attention to the words you use in the privacy of your own mind.

One of my daughters was struggling with her math homework. I spent some time helping her, with a computer program and by making flash cards together. While we worked together, I noticed she was saying mean things to herself. *Ugh, I'm so dumb. This is so hard. I can't do this. I'll never get all this right. I'm no good in math.*

Her words hurt my heart because I love her so much. And if God loves her far more than I do, can you imagine how her words sounded to Him? She was talking about one of His special creations in a way that suggested God had made some major mistakes. I asked my daughter if she would ever tell her body things before a race like *You'll never make it. You are going to quit. You are going to lose.*

"Of course not," she said.

"Okay then," I said. "So if you tell your body it's going to lose, it will lose. If you tell your brain it will fail, it will fail. We have to speak blessings to other people...and to ourselves." So I helped her change her words. Instead of, "This is too hard for me," she can say, "This is hard, but I love a challenge." Or instead of, "I'm terrible at this," she can say, "I'm working on this." Just making small changes to the words we speak on the inside can make big changes to the person we are becoming on the outside.

This week I want you to listen to the voice in your head. Notice the way you talk to yourself and the words you use. Are they words of encouragement and blessing? Or do you speak to yourself unkindly? If you have a journal, write down some of the things you tell yourself. Can you rewrite them in a better way? Can you start to talk to yourself in a kinder, more positive way?

The way we treat ourselves plays a big part in the way we treat other people.

Mother

> ...All you need to say is a simple "Yes" or "No." Otherwise you will be condemned.
>
> *James 5:12*

If you haven't spent any time studying the *Boundaries* books and workbooks by Henry Cloud and John Townsend, I recommend them highly. They are excellent tools for finding peace and priority in our own lives, and they are hugely helpful in parenting. Boundaries are the fence lines we maintain around our hearts, our homes, our families, and our relationships. They are the way that we guard our hearts, the wellspring of life (Prv 4:23). They are also the way we set limits for ourselves, as far as how we will allow other people to treat us. They are not a means of controlling others, but instead a deeper way of knowing and taking good care of ourselves.

We need to know our boundaries: what works for us, and what does not; what we appreciate, and what we don't; what matches our values, and what clashes with them; how far we are willing to go, and the certainty of what is too far. Boundary lines are the demarcation of a healthy "garden"; we know that what is inside is our responsibility and what lies beyond is not.

James is summarizing good boundaries in this verse. We need to know ourselves and our God well enough that we can confidently and clearly say yes or no when life presents a question. Our daughters present many questions, with many more difficult questions to come. We have to be able to communicate clearly where we stand. We have to be firm and loving. We have to be able to compromise without being compromised. Our daughters listen to our words, but they are also watching the way we live. Do our words and actions match our beliefs? Is our faith just fluff or is it our foundation? How do we treat people? How do we allow ourselves to be treated?

If we allow our boundaries to be twisted and reset, how will our daughters learn to create solid, healthy boundaries of their own? The biggest lesson of respect we can teach our girls is to treat others respectfully and mandate respectful treatment toward ourselves.

Take a look at your boundaries this week, your fence lines. Are they intentional and intact? Are you clear about your yeses and your noes? Are you able to set a limit peacefully and confidently and then enforce it in a firm and loving manner?

Look at the way you treat other people, and then look at the way you allow other people to treat you. Are you living freely and truthfully? Are you modeling healthy boundaries for your daughter?

How can you begin to firm up your fence lines this week?

Daughter

> ...All you need to say is a simple "Yes" or "No."
> Otherwise you will be condemned.
>
> *James 5:12*

It's easy to be wishy-washy, especially if we really don't know where we stand. There is an old saying that goes, "If you don't stand for something, you'll fall for anything." Boy, is that true.

And it becomes even more true the older you get, when what you say yes or no to can have consequences that change the rest of your life.

What you stand for has to do with your values. Your values are the things that you think are important, the things that define you. Some of our values come from our family and reflect the way we have been raised and what we believe. Other values come from our church or school and the messages we hear there. The close friends we spend time with can also shape our values. Of all these sources, our deepest values come directly from God. The more you know your values, the more you know yourself.

And when you really know yourself, you can be very clear when it comes to saying yes or no.

Sometimes you will say yes or no with your words, as

in, "Yes, I will do that," or "No, I will not." Other times you will say yes or no with your actions or your choices, and sometimes this speaks even louder than words. When you walk away from gossip, or talk to a new student who has no friends yet, or decide you don't want to watch a certain movie, or you stick up for someone who is being bullied—these are strong yes/no statements.

When you know what you believe and you know where you stand on certain things, it becomes easier to act according to your values. People always respect someone who knows who they are.

Take some time this week and journal some values that are important to you. If you are confused about values, talk to your mom about your family values and see which ones really mean something to you. How do you see yourself in the light of your values?

How can your yes and your no speak more clearly about who you are and who God is calling you to be? How can people know your values by the way you live?

Mother

May your unfailing love come to me, LORD...
Psalm 119:41

This verse is such comfort, tucked in our hearts, whispered in moments when we ache.

Feeling left out, uninvited, not chosen...when these feelings rush into your adult heart it can make you feel like you are still a child. It's a timeless feeling of unworthiness, and it hurts, plain and simple. It's good to feel it every once in a while so we can have fresh empathy for our daughters when they experience exclusion. If I can be honest about my own feelings, then I can use that awareness to guide, comfort, and strengthen my daughters when they feel left out. When I successfully use pain to point me back to God, then I can instruct my daughters to do likewise.

When we feel like we are left out or uninvited, we have to remind ourselves (and our daughters) that we are always chosen by God. He always wants our company, our connection, our time, and our heart. That knowledge can restore our sense of worth and our confidence. There are mean girls of all ages, and they exclude on purpose to feel powerful. There are also occasions when oversight or exclusion is for no malicious reason at all, and we must remember that we possess just as much freedom as the person sending the invitation we did not receive. We can find other things to do, with other people. When we are grateful and enjoying our own lives, we pay less attention to what other people are doing.

When we admit our aches to God, He rushes in and offers comfort—not the human comfort that placates or distracts, but the deep comfort that is His unfailing love. His unfailing love heals the wounds caused by failing love, and we are restored. No human being can comfort in this way because no human has the power to heal the heart. Some people make us feel better (and thank God for them too), but only God makes us better.

Sometimes we need to temporarily avoid painful people— especially if we are so vulnerable around them that we are consistently derailed. Other times we need to hold steady, examine the relationships that we allow to undermine us, and allow God to teach us. Sometimes the discomfort itself is a sign of healing, a sign of letting go, or a sign that we are ready to put our hope and our heart in safer hands.

Do you have certain relationships that cause you friction or discomfort? Do certain people always bring up old wounds? Have you ever considered that God is deliberately putting that person in your path in order to get you to look at the very thing you want to look away from? Admit weakness in order to receive strength.

Daughter

May your unfailing love come to me, LORD . . .
Psalm 119:41

This week I want to talk about the feeling of being left out.

It's a painful feeling, I know. No one really likes to admit it or talk about it. It hurts, it's embarrassing sometimes, and the funny thing is, it happens to everyone—not just girls, but grown-ups too. And not just shy people or awkward people—popular people feel it too. It hurts no matter how mature or how cool you think you are.

The thing is, no matter how good they are, human love and human relationships are imperfect. They fail us sometimes. There is only one relationship, one friendship, one love that will never let us down or leave us out—and that is the unfailing love of God.

When someone hurts our feelings, we have choices. We can become bitter and attempt to hurt them back. We can stuff our feelings deep inside and pretend we just don't care. We can talk to other people and use gossip to say bad things about someone else in order to make ourselves feel better. We can cry and stay in our room while everyone else is having fun. Or we can go to God.

This verse is a perfect way to reach out to God. Memorize

this verse and tuck it in your heart. At the exact moment you feel the sting of a hurt feeling, say this verse in your head. By proclaiming our faith that God's love is unfailing, we minimize the failing of another person—even ourselves. Admitting our weakness paves the way for God's strength to come into a situation, and into our heart, and change things.

Sometimes circumstances don't change. Sometimes other people don't change. They may continue to say things that hurt us. But what will always change is something within us. Our heart will change; certain things just won't hurt anymore. Our heads will change; God can change the way we think. Maybe some things won't seem as important and will no longer have power over us. Our actions will change; we can admit a hurt, yet release it and move on with our day.

Don't allow pain to make you bitter. Don't stuff hurt feelings deep inside and hope they will go away. Talk to God. Talk to someone you trust—your best friend, your sibling, your parent. Putting a feeling in the light always helps us see it clearly, and usually it isn't as huge or as horrible as we think. Most of all, we figure out that we don't have to deal with it alone. And this is the best comfort of all.

Lord, teach me to take my hurt feelings to You right away. Send Your unfailing love to me this week, and show me what Your help and healing can do. In Jesus' name, amen.

Mother

> ... This too is meaningless, a chasing after the
> wind.
>
> *Ecclesiastes 2:26*

I remember when I worked in the corporate world, our human resources department made us spend an afternoon in a session where we had to take a test. There were questions to answer that eventually placed you somewhere on a quadrant, signifying if you spent more time doing the wrong things right, the right things wrong, the wrong things wrong, or the right things right. Basically, how effective are you with your time?

God gives us twenty-four hours in a day. When we put Him first in the morning and ask Him to manage our time, we end up doing more right things right. He aligns our priorities so we don't waste time "chasing after wind." When we put the world first in the morning and exclude God from our plans, we might hit a few right things right, but we will definitely spend time in all the quadrants. Personally, if I am not properly aligned, I can spend plenty of time on my to-do list, which is often filled with opportunities to do the wrong things right. I may check off every single thing, but miss the most meaningful way I could have spent my time that day. My day was spent chasing after wind, seeking to glorify my own efficiency or accomplishment, not God.

Another word for chasing after wind is "striving." What do you strive for? Do you strive to be well liked or well received? Do you strive for accolades? Do you strive for beauty, youth, or a certain weight? Do you strive for approval? Do you strive for inclusion? Do you strive for certain achievements? Do you strive for material things? Do you strive for comfort?

The only purposeful striving is striving after God. If you want to chase after wind, then chase the Holy Spirit. You can accept this because it's true, or you can be like me and accept it by a painful process of elimination, trying all the other things first and then finding out what matters. Either way, you will come to the same peaceful and poignant conclusion.

Pull out your calendar and your checkbook (or pull up your Google Calendar and Quicken, however you roll) and try to pinpoint the wind you chase. See how you spend your time and your money, and this in-your-face summary will show you where and how you strive. Think about purposeful, meaningful striving, striving to know God better, to learn His Word, to live out His teaching, to share His message, to instruct our daughters, to refine our priorities, to find His will. Strive in that way—spend time doing the right things right.

Daughter

> ...This too is meaningless, a chasing after the wind.
>
> *Ecclesiastes 2:26*

When we chase after things that are not important to God, we may as well be chasing after the wind. Think about chasing the wind for just a second, running across the playground or a big field with your hands wide open, grasping...what? Something invisible that blows right through your fingers, impossible to outrun and impossible to grab.

The world tells us to chase after many things. It tells us to chase after beauty and buy certain clothes and makeup. It says to chase after popularity and approval, to do whatever it takes to be included, or accepted, or liked. The world says we should chase after material things and make sure we own whatever is cool. It encourages us to chase after love, success, and accomplishment. It urges us to chase after attention. And finally, we should chase after whatever anyone else happens to be chasing, regardless of if we really want it or not, if it's good for us or not.

When we chase after God, our chasing is meaningful. It is worth chasing to try to know Him better. It is meaningful to spend more time reading the Bible and understanding

His Word. It is worthy to pray and try to listen for answers. God says that all who seek Him will find Him, if they seek Him with all their heart.

This week I want you to think about the things you chase after. When you have some quiet time, make a list of them in your journal. Now rewrite them in two columns, one labeled **Wind** and one labeled **Worthy**. Notice how many things you have in each column—do you have more in one or the other?

Think about how you can spend more of your time chasing after things that are worthy. Think about how you can let the rest blow away.

> *Lord, help me to chase after the things that matter to You. Help me to seek You with all my heart and find You. I want a life that is meaningful, not meaningless. Help me to be more certain of what really matters, even if it looks different from other people's choices. Make me strong to look to You instead of the world. Help me to follow Your will instead of the wind. In Jesus' name I pray, amen.*

Mother

> "Go," said Jesus, "your faith has healed you."
> Immediately he received his sight and followed
> Jesus along the road.
>
> *Mark 10:52*

Oh, how I love that our God is a God of second chances!

For anyone who has ever been in desperate need of a do-over, you are probably smiling right along with me right now, nodding your head. Bartimaeus was a blind man, sitting by the side of the road, begging, when along comes his second chance—*Jesus*.

Bartimaeus hears that Jesus of Nazareth is nearby and starts screaming for the Son of David to have mercy on him. People try to shush him, but he is relentless in his pleas. I mean, how often do you get an opportunity for a second chance? Jesus goes over to him and asks, "What do you want me to do for you?"

"Rabbi, I want to see!"

And then, just like that, his second chance—Bartimaeus, the formerly blind beggar, could see!

Think of times in your life when you have been down on your luck and lacking vision. Maybe you are having one of those times right now? Jesus still asks us the very same question: "What do you want me to do for you?" He still offers the second chance. Do you know what your answer to His question is?

As soon as Bartimaeus can see, he gets up and follows Jesus. This teaches us what to do if we are blessed by a second chance—follow the One who gave it to us! I know people who have recovered from cancer, healed from a brain injury, recovered after an automobile accident, endured a rocky divorce and remarried, lost a child and had another baby, survived a heart attack—all these people have different stories, but the same theme. God gave them a second chance, a second chance to do things differently, to love generously, to live boldly, to follow Him fully.

This week think about the answer to Jesus' question, "What do you want me to do for you?" You might need some journal pages for this one. What do you really want? If you had a chance for a do-over, what would you do differently? If you suddenly had the gift of sight, what would be the first thing you would want to see?

When you have your answer, go to God boldly with your desire. Be relentless in your pursuit of Him. Be persistent in your prayer life. Ask Him to give you the desires of your heart—or to change your heart so that your desires match His.

Daughter

**"Go," said Jesus, "your faith has healed you."
Immediately he received his sight and followed
Jesus along the road.**

Mark 10:52

The story of Bartimaeus is one of persistence, or not giving up. Bartimaeus was a blind man, sitting and begging on the roadside just beyond the city of Jericho. He heard that Jesus was passing by and began to yell for Him to come and have mercy on him. People in the crowd, perhaps embarrassed by his yelling, tried to shush him. But Bartimaeus would not be quiet. He was persistent as he called out for Jesus.

Jesus, who never overlooks anyone in need, naturally stopped to talk to Bartimaeus. Bartimaeus knew this was his big opportunity for a second chance, and he was ready. Jesus asked him a very important question: "What do you want me to do for you?"

He responded quickly and certainly, asking for what you might imagine a blind man might want more than anything: "I want to see!" Bartimaeus was bold in his response. He didn't say, "Well, if it's possible, I'd really like it if maybe you could do something about my eyes." Or "If you can do anything about it, how about fixing my blindness?" There were no ifs or maybes when it came to what Bartimaeus thought Jesus could do. He had a chance to ask God's Son for help, and he went for it!

Bartimaeus was able to see immediately! And what was the first thing he did as soon as he had eyesight? He followed Jesus!

As soon as he got his second chance, he made the most of it by following Jesus. As soon as he could see, he kept his eyes on the One worth watching.

You and I have the same option to have a second chance, no matter what mistakes we've made or what odds we have stacked against us. We can ask Jesus for what we really want and be as bold as Bartimaeus.

If Jesus asked you, this week, the same question—"What do you want me to do for you?"—what would your answer be? In other words, what is the desire of your heart? You can pray to Jesus and be just as close to Him as Bartimaeus was, sitting on the side of the road as He walked by. He wants to heal the things that hurt, He wants to offer hope when you feel hopeless, and most of all He wants to help you so that the desires of your heart match what He desires for you.

If you could have a second chance at anything—what would it be? And if you got that fresh start, what would you do first?

Mother

> I consider that our present sufferings are not worth comparing with the glory that will be revealed in us.
>
> *Romans 8:18*

Pain is the catalyst for growth. We have to get uncomfortable enough that we are willing to take a risk and learn to do something new or different. No season of suffering is pointless, no matter how much it feels that way. God is always after something when He prunes His people.

Before I experienced a season of misery resulting from my own sin and disobedience, I couldn't imagine how anyone could be so foolish or selfish. I was so righteous because I had not yet felt the real shock at how easily I could be deceived, or how quickly one slip of integrity can cause an avalanche. Now, because of that season, I judge less and love more. I have compassion and I have the ability to speak the truth to those who are sliding because I know what it's like to fall.

Because of that season of suffering in my life, I am able to love in a whole new way, a way that brings glory to God. We have to hurt to learn about healing. We have to fail to learn forgiveness. We experience ruin to learn repentance. We survive loss in order to fully love.

If you are in a season of suffering, hang in and hang on because you will get to the other side and His glory will be revealed. Cooperate with God in your pruning and you will be transformed and more useful than you can imagine. Our culture reveres comfort so much that we will do anything to avoid suffering. We even go to the extent of avoiding those who suffer, in case pain is contagious. We are so afraid to hurt or allow anyone we love to hurt.

If suffering yields growth, let's stop labeling it "bad." It just is what it is. If we learn to endure our present sufferings with grace and hopefulness, His glory is revealed much sooner. We don't help our daughters grow if all we teach are tactics to avoid suffering or if we always cushion their consequences.

Lord, I love my daughter so much that I want to protect her, even when it's not my place to do so. Help me know when to step in and when to step back, and when the lesson is Yours to teach. Help me to face my own challenges squarely and not be intimidated by the discomfort that leads to growth. I know I can endure anything with You by my side. I want to grow, and I want to live a life that encourages growth in those I love. My heart is willing, but I am weak. Manifest Your strength and wisdom in me. In Jesus' name, amen.

Daughter

> I consider that our present sufferings are not
> worth comparing with the glory that will be
> revealed in us.
>
> *Romans 8:18*

We've studied enough Scripture together this year to know that sometimes God allows us to suffer.

He doesn't intend to hurt us or make us miserable—remember, God is good to the core, and even when we don't understand His ways, they are always meant to teach us and prepare us for the future. We can't fully understand His plan because it's too big and it involves everyone, not just us.

What if we pray for very important things, things we think are good, and we don't get what we want? What if God doesn't heal our family member's cancer? What if our grandmother dies? What if our parents get divorced, no matter how hard we prayed they wouldn't? What if our dog gets hit by a car? These are hard things, and this is what Paul means in this Scripture when he talks about "present sufferings." Suffering like this can cause us either to draw near to God or to get angry and turn away from Him.

It's okay to be angry with God—He can handle it—as

long as we don't *stay angry*. We can't turn away forever from the only One who can heal and help us. When we turn to God for comfort, He teaches us things in our suffering that He could not teach us any other way. Good and easy times are fun, but we are usually too distracted to learn as much as we do when times are tough. Hard times remind us of how much we need God. When we turn to God in our suffering, our pain is never worthless—He always uses it to change us in a way that His glory shines through us.

Suffering teaches us things that we can later use to help other people who struggle with similar things. For example, if your parents get divorced, once God helps you heal, you can comfort and help other friends who suffer after you. Or if you once moved to a new school and didn't know anyone, you can later help someone else who feels lost or alone. If you never suffered, you would have no compassion for other people when they hurt. God softens your heart so you can recognize other people's pain and want to help them.

How can you use your experiences to help someone else right now? Do you know anyone who is struggling with a pain that you understand? How can you reach out to them this week to let them know you care?

You give thanks and glory to God every time you help another one of His children.

Mother

> LORD, you alone are my portion and my cup; you make my lot secure. The boundary lines have fallen for me in pleasant places; surely I have a delightful inheritance. I will praise the LORD, who counsels me; even at night my heart instructs me. I keep my eyes always on the LORD. With him at my right hand, I will not be shaken.
>
> *Psalm 16:5–8*

We've been on this journey together for a year now. I prayed for the past two days for God to show me how He wants me to close this book. This morning, I opened right to this verse, and I knew it was my answer. And speaking of answers, the more we learn and experience, the more we realize something about answers—namely, we don't have any! The point of our journey is to recognize this simple, humbling fact and set our minds instead to learning how to ask better questions.

As soon as we think we know ourselves, we are surprised (sometimes shocked) by a new revelation (*I can't believe I did that!* or *I can't believe I can do that!*). As soon as we think we've got this parenting gig down, our children grow to a new level and we are back to clueless again. As soon as we think we are beginning to understand God, He pulls a fast one and reminds us that He is the master of mystery and can never be understood. So we go about seeking Him instead.

That is why this verse is so perfect. It feels like it comes from a mother's heart. We are grateful for the gifts of our portion (our families) and our cup (our provision). We continue to work on good boundaries, and we put our hope in God that He has a good future and a plan for us and for our daughters. We don't know the answers, but we are good students who realize the more we know, the more we don't know. We want to learn and grow, and that is the key. We receive our counsel from the Lord because although we don't have answers, He surely does. The Lord lights the path of our parenting, and we follow His lead. He will not leave us or forsake us.

We will not be shaken.

The world may shake us; in fact, circumstances may turn us upside down. But at our core, we can and we will be steady. And in a highly unsteady world, the best gift we can give our daughters is to be unshakable.

Father, we thank You for the journey of this year, these fifty-two weeks of traveling through Your Word. Because Your Word is alive, we cannot emerge unchanged. Continue this good work You started in our hearts. Help us to be who You want us to be and do what You call us to do. Strengthen us for the road ahead, and sustain us as we go. Bless our daughters, fortify their generation, and help us build a legacy on the foundation of Your great love. In Your Son's name we pray, amen.

Daughter

> LORD, you alone are my portion and my cup; you make my lot secure. The boundary lines have fallen for me in pleasant places; surely I have a delightful inheritance. I will praise the LORD, who counsels me; even at night my heart instructs me. I keep my eyes always on the LORD. With him at my right hand, I will not be shaken.
>
> *Psalm 16:5–8*

Oh sweet girl, I have loved sharing a whole year of faith with you. I hope you have grown and changed and seeds have taken root in the good soil of your heart. Keep planting more good seeds and taking good care of that garden. Water it with living water, stay in the light, be grateful for the seasons, and pull weeds as soon as you see them—don't delay.

You do have a delightful inheritance because your real inheritance is your faith. It is being passed from your mother into you, and one day you will pass it on too. But faith is a very personal thing; it is *your own* relationship with God and Jesus. So when you are young you may believe what your parents believe, but God wants you to grow and believe *Him*. This is a real and grown-up faith, and this will be your portion and your cup. This will be your secure lot.

Just as your mom doesn't always know what to do, there will be moments ahead when you are at a crossroads and you don't know what to do. Decisions, big and small, await you; what you decide will determine your character and the direction of your life. Your mom is there for you, but even she can't be with you 100 percent of the time. But God is, and He will counsel you. If you set Him and His ways before you, you will always figure out what to do. And when you make mistakes, accept His grace, dust off, and get back on track.

Although the world may be shaky, you, my dear, will not be shaken. You have a solid, sacred core that the world cannot disturb. Keep it holy. Keep it real. Keep it alive.

God is with you, and the prayers of many faithful women join you on your journey. This is my prayer for you:

Father,

Bless this child. Hold her lovely face in your hands and turn her gaze toward You. Remind her that she is Your daughter. *She has been chosen by You; she is spoken for and cherished. She can do no wrong that You cannot forgive. There is no place she can wander where You cannot find her. Anoint her with a deep and abiding faith, and pour Your peace into her. Protect her, guide her, encourage her, and love her—as only You can love. In the name of the Father, Son, and Holy Spirit, amen.*